W9-BTE-885

American Foreign Relations: A Very Short Introduction

VERY SHORT INTRODUCTIONS are for anyone wanting a stimulating and accessible way into a new subject. They are written by experts, and have been translated into more than 45 different languages.

The series began in 1995, and now covers a wide variety of topics in every discipline. The VSI library currently contains over 550 volumes—a Very Short Introduction to everything from Psychology and Philosophy of Science to American History and Relativity—and continues to grow in every subject area.

Very Short Introductions available now:

For more information visit our web site

www.oup.com/vsi/

Andrew Preston

AMERICAN
FOREIGN
RELATIONS

A Very Short Introduction

OXFORD
UNIVERSITY PRESS

OXFORD
UNIVERSITY PRESS

Oxford University Press is a department of the University of Oxford.
It furthers the University's objective of excellence in research, scholarship,
and education by publishing worldwide. Oxford is a registered trade mark of
Oxford University Press in the UK and certain other countries.

Published in the United States of America by Oxford University Press
198 Madison Avenue, New York, NY 10016, United States of America.

© Oxford University Press 2019

All rights reserved. No part of this publication may be reproduced,
stored in a retrieval system, or transmitted, in any form or by any means,
without the prior permission in writing of Oxford University Press,
or as expressly permitted by law, by license, or under terms agreed with
the appropriate reproduction rights organization. Inquiries concerning
reproduction outside the scope of the above should be sent to the
Rights Department, Oxford University Press, at the address above.

You must not circulate this work in any other form
and you must impose this same condition on any acquirer.

Library of Congress Cataloging-in-Publication Data
Names: Preston, Andrew, 1973- author.
Title: American foreign relations : a very short introduction /
Andrew Preston.
Description: New York, NY : Oxford University Press, [2019] |
Series: Very short introductions | Includes bibliographical
references and index.
Identifiers: LCCN 2018050206 (print) | LCCN 2018050652 (ebook) |
ISBN 9780199899517 (updf) | ISBN 9780190946029 (epub) |
ISBN 9780199899395 (pbk. : alk. paper)
Subjects: LCSH: United States—Foreign relations.
Classification: LCC E744 (ebook) | LCC E744 .P743 2019 (print) |
DDC 327.73—dc23
LC record available at https://lccn.loc.gov/2018050206

Printed by Integrated Books International, United States of America
on acid-free paper

Contents

List of illustrations

Acknowledgments

The task of compressing such a huge topic into such a short space has been enjoyable but challenging. For their help in making suggestions, providing a careful reading, and saving me from embarrassing mistakes, I would like to thank Kate Epstein, Nick Guyatt, Andy Rotter, John Thompson, and an extremely helpful report by an anonymous reader. Any remaining errors are my own. Finally, I would like to thank my editor, Susan Ferber, for her stoic patience, insightful and careful editing, and cheerful encouragement.

Introduction

The history of American foreign relations should be of interest to any person from any country. This is because, unlike any other great power since the beginning of the twentieth century, the United States has affected the history of virtually every other country in the world. So great has the United States' presence been—culturally, economically, politically, technologically, militarily—that how it conducts its relations with the rest of the world is of unusually wide global relevance. To a significant extent, for better or worse, we all inhabit a world created by American values, systems, technologies, and power; and, in turn, by the adoption of and resistance to these American phenomena. Understanding the history of American foreign relations is therefore key to understanding the world we all live in.

This is not to say that America in the world has been omnipotent or its influence determinative. As powerful as the United States has been, it has failed to get its way on many occasions. Yet even then—in Vietnam or Iraq, for example—the consequences have been impossible to ignore. Nor is this to say that the United States' foreign interactions have always been beneficial—to say that the United States' power is great doesn't necessarily mean that it's always been good.

For these reasons, there is a great deal of controversy surrounding the topic of American foreign relations. This very short introduction on such a large and important subject aims to address, in as even-handed a manner as possible, some of the most important topics and common myths about the United States in the world.

First, a word on terminology. I use the term "history of foreign relations" here deliberately, instead of the most common alternative label, "diplomatic history." This is because "foreign relations" is more capacious and inclusive, incorporating not only state policy, military strategy, and high diplomacy, but also non-state interactions stemming from trade, immigration, religious missions, and culture. Given that America's global footprint has often had little to do with diplomats and strategists in Washington, "foreign relations," which includes both international history from the top down and transnational history from the bottom up, seems more appropriate and accurate.

In highlighting many of the key moments in American foreign-relations history, this book is animated by seven key themes, many of which are, at various points, mutually reinforcing.

First is the importance of values and a sense of mission. All great powers are motivated by their ideals, but American foreign relations have been to an unusual degree moralistic and normative. This is because a belief that the United States is special and thus has a special role to play—an ideology known as "exceptionalism"—has been an inordinately large influence in determining US interests in the world.

Second, ideas about expansion and progress have played a critical role in how Americans envision the world around them. At first, this had a literal meaning in the form of territorial acquisition, but expansion and progress have also meant the spread of American values, driven by a desire to change the external world around the

United States not just for the benefit of Americans, but also for the benefit of others. In other words, progress *required* expansion. Whether non-Americans welcomed American progress is sometimes questionable, but it's also, when determining what motivated Americans in the first place, beside the point.

Third, race, gender, and religion have been particularly potent sources of American engagement with the world. The United States was founded as a white, slaveholding republic with Protestantism and manhood as key pillars of political culture. Those who traditionally lacked power—African Americans, women, Catholics, Jews, Mormons—had to conform to the norms established by white male Protestants. Over time, this power dynamic shifted, as American society became more pluralistic and as the world decolonized. Yet the authority of these longstanding norms has remained remarkably durable.

Shift to equality

Fourth is the centrality of war to the American experience—not just the American experience abroad, but American history itself. Two of the most pervasive national myths are that the United States wages war infrequently and that it is slow to go to war. In reality, Americans have often resorted to armed force to achieve their goals, at first on the North American continent and then around the world. In fact, over the past 250 years, warfare is perhaps the most consistent aspect of American foreign relations, and it has had a deep and lasting impact on the evolution of American culture, economics, social norms, and political institutions. By the same token, this shouldn't lead us to perceive the United States as an unusually aggressive, warmongering state, but rather as a nation like any other: no more aggressive, but also no less.

internally & externally

Fifth, the basic geographical position of the United States has had a profound but usually overlooked importance on its foreign relations. It is surrounded on all sides by an absence of threat, and has been for almost its entire history. This is what historians refer to as "free security." Since the end of the War of 1812, the United States hasn't faced a threat of foreign invasion, much less occupation. Over the same period, all of its great-power competitors have had precisely that experience, sometimes repeatedly, and only Britain has actually escaped invasion and occupation. The advent of transoceanic air power and nuclear energy in the 1940s complicated American security, but they didn't negate the nation's geographical good fortune. While Americans have come under foreign attack (not least on September 11, 2001), those instances, while horrific, have been exceptional.

Sixth is the pernicious myth of "isolationism." There has never been a time in American history when Americans simply kept to themselves in isolation, and free security didn't mean that the United States was somehow sealed off from the rest of the world. As long as there has been a United States, Americans have roamed the planet in search of commerce and converts, while the persistence of warfare reflects a darker side of American engagement with the rest of the world. However, it is certainly the case that Americans acted "unilaterally"—that is, within the world, but on their own terms—for much of their history, until the era of the world wars and the Cold War. This wasn't the same as "isolationism," a polemical term which first became widespread as a political epithet during the debate over intervention in World War II. The reason "isolationism" is pernicious is not only its highly politicized nature; it also allows Americans to believe in a non-existent golden age when matters were less complicated and Americans controlled their own destiny.

Seventh, finally, is the importance of domestic politics to the conduct of American foreign relations, including diplomacy and military intervention. Partly because of America's longstanding culture of popular democracy, and partly because free security removed the pressure of constant struggle for national survival, American war and diplomacy have been shaped by the need for popular and political legitimacy. Even when policymakers wanted to ignore popular pressures, they couldn't. Moreover, the decentralized structure of American governance—federalism as well as a system of divided government grounded in checks and balances and the separation of powers—has provided an almost infinite variety of opportunities for individuals and groups to lobby elected officials, and in turn for those elected officials to lobby policymakers.

These seven themes are not exhaustive, but when I have considered the history of American engagement with the rest of the world, they have always struck me as useful signposts. They act first and foremost as interpretive lenses that can be used on their own or, if the picture is particularly complex or unclear, by overlaying one or more on top of another. They are also interrelated. For instance, free security's autonomy to choose a foreign policy not based on preventing invasion and occupation helps explain why both values and domestic politics have wielded such a heavy influence over such a long period of time.

Chapter 1
First principles

today s continues this >

The United States began its existence as an act of foreign policy—indeed, it's no exaggeration to say that the nation owes its very existence to the successful pursuit of war and diplomacy. Over a period of forty years, from the outbreak of revolution in 1775 to the end of war with Britain in 1815, the founding generation established and consolidated a new nation by responding to a series of international challenges. Along the way, they established a set of first principles of foreign relations—namely, unilateralism, exceptionalism, and expansionism—that would shape Americans' engagement with the wider world for centuries to come.

The new republic

Until the mid-1770s, the residents of what would become the United States were subjects of the British Crown, and considered a part of the British Empire. It took a series of imperial crises to stimulate demands for independence on the part of the American colonies. In 1763, after defeating France in the Seven Years' War, Britain became the dominant European power over the eastern half of North America. In order to maintain peace with American Indians, who still inhabited most of the continent, British officials established the Proclamation Line along the spine of the Appalachian Mountains and prohibited colonial settlement beyond it. A few years later, they began to tax the North American colonists for the costs of war with France. Both measures infuriated the colonists, who considered westward expansion as both a natural right and an economic necessity. British authorities cracked down on dissent, further agitating rebellious sentiment. After tensions escalated in the early 1770s, with British measures such as the so-called Intolerable Acts and the Quebec Act provoking increasingly furious protests, war broke out in Massachusetts, in the spring of 1775, with the battles of Concord and Lexington.

The decisive break with Britain came a year later, when the Continental Congress gathered in Philadelphia to present and sign the Declaration of Independence. The Declaration's main purpose was to unite more firmly what had been until then a loose collective of disparate and often disputatious individual colonies—in other words, to form a new, independent union. The authors of the Declaration wanted their new nation "to assume among the powers of the earth" a "separate and equal station." But to do that, they needed to defeat the British, which required allies. Thus, another of the Declaration's objectives was to appeal to Britain's rivals in Europe, especially France, and demonstrate that there was now no turning back from revolution. Appealing to "a decent respect to the opinions of mankind," the rebels sought to air their grievances with Britain and "let Facts be submitted to a candid world." The Declaration of Independence, then, was a call for assistance as much as it was a demonstration of resolve.

In launching the American Revolution, the colonists needed to balance their ambitions for national independence with the need to forge military and diplomatic ties with Britain's rivals, France and Spain. On one hand, foreign alliances were vital: the British possessed the most powerful military in the world; the Royal Navy alone was powerful enough to make life difficult for the United States; and ever since the Seven Years' War the British had had a large presence of troops in North America. There was little chance that the new United States would succeed without partners and support—indeed, the Continental Congress already was smuggling in large quantities of arms and materiel from continental Europe. On the other hand, if the rebels promised too much to the French and the Spanish, the forging of alliances could undermine the very independence for which the colonists were fighting.

John Adams, a Massachusetts lawyer and one of the leading figures of the American Revolution, thought he had found a way to align with partners while retaining American autonomy. In 1776, he drafted the Model Treaty, which provided a template for the new nation's foreign relations. Adams believed that the new nation could not survive as a vassal of one of the European powers; a product of Puritan New England, he was also deeply anti-Catholic and distrustful of monarchy. Shaped by the unavoidable specter of France's power, but designed nonetheless to be an enduring blueprint for the role of the United States in the world, the Model Treaty set out to prevent Americans from becoming entangled in the political affairs of foreign allies, especially their squabbles with other countries. Adams prioritized commerce on the assumption that the new nation required foreign trade for its survival, but he made sure to avoid any permanent political or military commitments, such as indefinite non-aggression or mutual-assistance pacts in the event of war. This was a kind of declaration of independence in world affairs, the earliest expression of American unilateralism, and it was no coincidence that the Continental Congress had commissioned it as part of the deliberations that produced the Declaration. Yet for now, the French were wary of an open partnership with the rebels, and not quite ready for an open confrontation with London.

The first two years of the Revolutionary War were difficult for both sides; neither the British nor the Americans could sustain enough momentum to mount a winning campaign. After short-lived American victories, Boston, a stronghold of anti-British agitation, was trapped under siege for nearly a year while

British generals won a series of battles around New York City and pursued the main American army, under the command of George Washington, into New Jersey. Washington was able to stem the British advance at Trenton and Princeton in December 1776 and January 1777, respectively, but his troops had suffered tremendously. The first major American victory didn't come until the fall of 1777, when soldiers surrounded British General John Burgoyne and his troops near Saratoga, New York, and forced their surrender.

The British, by most measurements the stronger side, were becoming increasingly frustrated at their inability to quell the insurgency. Yet despite Saratoga, the war was far from over. From an American standpoint, the campaign for independence had scored some notable triumphs, but ultimate success was still uncertain. The Americans thus had little choice but to cement an alliance with France, which was eager to weaken Britain's power and prestige and earn a measure of revenge for the Seven Years' War. An alliance with France may have been necessary, but for the rebel government the trick was to maintain American independence, not only from Britain but also from the demands of its new sponsors in Paris. Burgoyne's surrender at Saratoga, following the Declaration of Independence, convinced the French that the American rebellion was credible.

The Franco-American alliance, a secret up to that point, could now come out into the open. Contrary to Adams's designs, the diplomatic mission to Paris, headed by Benjamin Franklin, had to make some uncomfortable promises. The Model Treaty was supposed to be adaptable to different circumstances, but the underlying premise—that America must avoid becoming entangled in foreign commitments—was pragmatically sacrificed to the urgent need for an alliance with France. Franklin didn't have to give away too much, however—a vow not to sign a separate peace with Britain and a promise to help France recover lost territories in the Caribbean—and the Franco-American alliance was sealed in February 1778. This was a decisive moment: alone against Britain, the Americans were unlikely to prevail, at least in the near term, but in partnership with France, which could also apply pressure elsewhere in the world, the American insurgency had every chance of success. Encouraged by the French, Spain and the Netherlands joined the campaign against Britain, while other European nations, among them Russia, Sweden, Denmark, Prussia, and Portugal, undermined the British blockade of North America by maintaining neutral shipping and trading rights.

The Revolutionary War lasted eight years, ending only with the surrender of British forces at Yorktown, Virginia, in 1781 and the signing of a peace treaty in Paris in 1783. European intervention was important, with French forces proving especially critical right up to the battle of Yorktown. With the signing of the Treaty of Paris, the United States was recognized, even by Great Britain, as a sovereign state in the international system. The aims of the Declaration of Independence had been met. The United States could now claim, in theory, as much legitimacy as any other state, including Britain itself.

Out of many

The legitimacy of the United States, however, existed only on paper, and it was immediately apparent that the country lacked something else just as important: power. Partly this was due to the nature of the newly independent American states, which assumed that they would be acting more or less as autonomous bodies in a loose confederation, rather than as subject to, and part of, a centrally organized single national body. Potentially strong in the aggregate, they were actually quite weak as a collective. It wasn't as if the leaders of the Revolution had forgotten about the needs of national governance. Even as fighting raged during the Revolutionary War, the Continental Congress had been busy erecting a framework for a new government, called the Articles of

Confederation. But by providing for a weak central government that lacked an executive or taxing authority, the Articles reflected the former colonies' desire to protect their autonomy. The problem of "thirteen sovereignties pulling against each other, and all tugging at the federal head," Washington warned James Madison in 1786, threatened to undermine national cohesion from the very start. The new states couldn't negotiate treaties or enter into a foreign war on their own, but nor could Congress negotiate treaties with other countries that would affect the rights or individual American states. It was an unworkable system of government.

More to the point, it was also a dangerous one, particularly for an upstart republic that was economically dependent on overseas trade. On land and at sea, the United States was beset by foreigners encroaching on their sovereignty. By the peace terms signed in 1783, Britain had agreed to cede all territorial claims west to the Mississippi River, south to Spanish Florida, and north to the Great Lakes. This essentially doubled the size of the nation as originally constituted by the original thirteen colonies, and meant that Congress had a huge swathe of additional territory to defend—isolated, sparsely populated territory at that. In the south, the Spanish, who had not signed the Treaty of Paris, disputed US land claims. In the north, the British may have relinquished territory, but their troops remained on what was now, legally, US soil. And throughout the United States, to the north, south, and in the west, American Indians fiercely contested attempts by the new national government to exert its authority.

These problems of sovereignty were compounded by the ceaseless migration of white, Anglophone settlers westward—it's probably inaccurate to refer to them collectively as "Americans," even after 1783, because their loyalty to the United States was uncertain and often tenuous. As settlers poured over the Appalachians into what are now the states of Ohio, Kentucky, and Tennessee, they came into conflict with American Indians, who in turn were encouraged and supplied by the British and the Spanish. All through the 1780s, warfare was constant along the trans-Appalachian borderlands.

The situation was little better at sea. The thirteen colonies had long prospered from economic relations with other nations, and maritime commerce was essential to American prosperity—without it, the viability of the United States was doubtful. American merchants and shippers had always benefitted from the protective blanket of Britain's Royal Navy, which was now, at best, an unsympathetic neutral. Without protection, American ships fell prey to pirates and privateers. Their most frequent predators were raiders from the Barbary states of North Africa (essentially what are now the countries of Morocco, Algeria, Tunisia, and Libya), which harassed and captured US ships in the Mediterranean and the eastern Atlantic. Ransom payments freed the ships and their crews, but did nothing to discourage further raids. Even when ships sailing under the US flag avoided attack, they found that British and Spanish colonial ports were closed to them.

With no standing army at its disposal, no navy to speak of, and no authority to raise taxes, Congress was powerless to defend the United States from outside attackers. Without an effective central coordinating body to oversee the nation's foreign or military policies, Congress also had trouble promoting its national interests, such as free trade and neutral shipping that would help overcome the protective mercantilist barriers that barred Americans from lucrative trade routes in the Caribbean. Although the State Department had technically come into existence, it was a toothless body left to the mercy of the whims of the individual states.

In fact, under the Articles of Confederation, the United States couldn't really have a foreign policy. "Have we valuable territories and important posts in the possession of a foreign power which, by express stipulations, ought long since to have been surrendered?" an exasperated Alexander Hamilton asked readers of the *Federalist Papers*. Thanks to British and Spanish predations in the Great Lakes and the Southwest, the answer was painfully obvious. "Are we in a condition to resent or to repel the aggression?" The answer, again, was just as clear: "We have neither troops, nor treasury, nor government."

Without a foreign policy, America's ability to operate as an independent nation in the world was compromised. But much more than trade was at stake: the very survival of the United States was in question. If it couldn't fend off or even deter British, Spanish, and American Indians along its extensive land borders; if it couldn't legally gain access to maritime European trade; and if it couldn't protect itself against Barbary pirates, then the United States would likely fall apart due to foreign land grabs, American Indian warfare, and secessionist movements.

Hamilton's searching questions reflected broader concerns about the nation's standing in the world. To overcome American weakness abroad, which was also eroding national cohesion within the new country, in 1787 Congress authorized the drafting of a new national constitution. This would, the Founders hoped, legitimize the upstart United States in the eyes of skeptical Europeans (even those sympathetic to the American republic doubted it could survive for very long). As the historian Eliga Gould puts it, a new constitution that enabled a more stable and centralized government would make the new nation "treaty-worthy," that is, a country with which other countries could do business. Without that legitimacy, Americans would be left vulnerable in the world. Foreign policy concerns weren't the only motivation behind the decision to replace the Articles of Confederation with a new constitution, but they were among the most important.

When drafting was finished, the Constitution provided for a much stronger central government, including a chief executive (the president) who would serve as commander-in-chief, and a strong legislature (Congress) that could raise taxes and collect customs and duties, and thus fund a proper military. Guided by Madison's theories of federalism, in which the executive and legislative branches would have separate but overlapping powers, the president and Congress both had oversight of foreign affairs and national defense. Only Congress could declare war, but once the armed forces were deployed the president was in charge. Only the president (and his cabinet officials) could negotiate treaties with foreign governments, but the Senate had the sole power of ratification and could thus veto any treaty the president signed. The president could appoint anyone to serve as secretary of state or war, but they too had to be confirmed by the Senate, giving the legislature a large voice in foreign affairs.

Over time, but especially in the twentieth century, the balance of power between the branches of government tilted increasingly in favor of the executive. The Founders felt the nation couldn't survive without stronger mechanisms for the United States to defend itself and advance its interests. Is the incredible power of the American presidency in the early twenty-first century the end result of pirate raids off the coast of northwest Africa two hundred and fifty years ago? That would be an exaggeration, but not by much.

Navigating a world at war

Whatever future problems lay in store, the Constitution, ratified and put into effect in 1789, placed America's relations with the rest of the world on firmer ground. However, that's not to say events proceeded smoothly and without crisis. From the outset, the 1790s presented immensely difficult, systemic challenges, as the United States found itself caught between the two superpowers of the day, Britain and France, and the war they fought, almost without interruption, until the final defeat of Napoleon in 1815. This was an important time in the history of American foreign relations because, in navigating between the British and the French, the founding generation entrenched their first principles of unilateralism and exceptionalism.

The alliance with France that was so critical to winning the Revolutionary War began to fray even as the ink was still drying on the Treaty of Paris, and by the outbreak of the French Revolution in 1789 it had reached a breaking point. Americans initially hailed the outbreak of revolution across the Atlantic: it seemed as if the French had learned from the American example. But the US government found dealing with Louis XVI had been easy by comparison. Tensions came to the fore in 1793, when a war that pitted France against the anti-revolutionary partnership of Austria and Prussia spread to the Low Countries. Britain joined the anti-French coalition. France, looking to harass and distract the British in the Western Hemisphere and hoping to recover some of its lost territory in North America and the Caribbean, called upon the United States to fulfill the obligations of the 1778 alliance.

Despite his Model Treaty, John Adams's nightmare had come to pass: the United States had become entangled in European politics and had, as a result, lost its own geopolitical freedom. Americans were naturally sympathetic to the French, and the memories of war with Britain were still fresh. But the United States needed trade, more specifically maritime-born trade with Western Europe and the Caribbean, and that meant abiding as much as possible by the wishes of the British, who had the most powerful naval force and the largest extent of colonies. In fact, the outbreak of yet another Anglo-French war, one that quickly enveloped all of Europe and spread across much of the globe, offered American merchants an unparalleled economic opportunity. For reasons of security and expediency, George Washington issued a declaration of neutrality. Acting unilaterally, the United States would trade with all and prejudice its relations with none.

That, at least, was Washington's intention. The main problem with unilateralism and neutrality was that it was beneficial to the United States but detrimental to both the British and the French, who insisted that Americans couldn't trade with both sides on equal terms. The French naturally demanded that the Americans abide by the terms of their treaty; the British, backed by the Royal Navy and dominant in the Americans' own region, insisted otherwise.

The issue of whether to side with Britain or France—partisans of both nations saw genuine neutrality as a capitulation to the other side—consumed American public life in the 1790s. Against the wishes and intentions of nearly every contributor to the Constitution, squabbling over Britain and France stimulated deep political divisions, giving rise to political factions that quickly congealed into the first party system: Hamilton and the Federalists were sympathetic to Britain and fairly conservative in their political ideology; Thomas Jefferson and the then-Republicans were Francophiles drawn to the radical republicanism and anti-clericalism of the French Revolution.

The two factions did have one important thing in common, however: both Hamiltonians and Jeffersonians shared a firm belief in the sanctity of neutral shipping and trading rights. This meant that the United States, as a non-belligerent in the revolutionary wars in Europe, claimed the freedom to trade with all parties, whether or not they were in a state of war, so long as they were not at war with the United States, even if trade actually benefitted one of the belligerents over another. This assertion of neutral rights effectively nullified the formal alliance with Paris—it was as if the French had signed Adams's Model Treaty of 1776, rather than the pact they actually agreed to in 1778. But for now, tensions were postponed by the mutually reinforcing facts that the French needed food and supplies and the Americans needed customers. By the mid-1790s, trade was flourishing between the two republics.

This immediately put the United States at odds with Great Britain, and sparked a crisis that eventually helped provoke a full-scale war in 1812. War didn't seem all that far off in 1794, when the long, transatlantic crisis over sovereign rights began. Customs officials in Britain's Caribbean ports and officers on Royal Navy ships seized Americans and their goods, without compensation but often with imprisonment. Trade with France was obviously affected, and with it American livelihoods—but perhaps even more damaging was the blow to US prestige and pride. More than a decade after the end of the American Revolution and the establishment of the United States of America, the British were still treating Americans little better than colonial subjects. Compounding matters were the continuing disputes over sovereignty in the Great Lakes region, with Britain and its American Indian allies refusing to acknowledge US rule and Americans unable to enforce it.

The crisis of 1794 led to a war scare, which in turn prompted a frustrated but anxious President Washington, who feared that war with Britain would lead to a calamitous defeat and perhaps the new country's breakup, to negotiate a settlement. He dispatched John Jay, who had acted as a kind of foreign minister for Congress in the 1780s and was now the first-ever Chief Justice of the Supreme Court, to London. Jay was a descendant of Huguenots, French Protestants who had fled for their lives in the late seventeenth century, first to England and then to the American colonies; like his fellow Federalists, he distrusted France, whether it was run by conservative Catholics or radical revolutionaries. The treaty he negotiated and signed in London betrayed some of these feelings toward Britain and France, but it also reflected the precarious economic and military position in which the United States found itself.

As an act of peacemaking, the Jay Treaty had a paradoxical effect: it soothed tensions with London while aggravating political grievances in the United States. On the whole, Jay's actions were unpopular; Republicans denounced him as a traitor, and even many Federalists struggled to defend him. In London, Jay conceded Britain's position on neutral shipping rights—there were none in a time of war—which was as significant a concession as possible for an American diplomat. In exchange, he secured from Britain a promise to vacate all territory east of the Mississippi River and south of the Great Lakes, to abandon tacit anti-American alliances with American Indians in the region, and to provide compensation for seized American goods and ships. In other words, Jay gave way on one of the most important principles of the new republic in return for Britain's promises to abide by the terms of a treaty it had already signed eleven years earlier. If it didn't seem like much of a bargain for the United States, it wasn't. But Jay had probably done as well as possible under the circumstances: war was averted, trade with Britain and its colonies boomed again, and a great power and former adversary had dealt with the United States as an equal.

The French didn't exactly see it that way. Incensed by both the Americans' unilateral abrogation of the 1778 treaty and the sharp increase in US trade with the British, France quickly replaced Britain as America's main adversary. With the ratification of the Jay Treaty in 1795, the French navy began harassing US ships and seizing their goods, and French diplomats ominously hinted at an impending war. Passions were further inflamed when John Adams, who succeeded Washington as president in 1797, sent a delegation to Paris to negotiate a truce. They were instead approached by three agents of the French government, known only by the codenames X, Y, and Z, who said that an immediate cash payment and a further loan would convince France to settle. The XYZ affair offended Americans' republican honor, and Adams recalled his negotiators with nothing to show for their efforts but wounded pride. Open naval conflict, known by the inelegant but accurate name of the Quasi-War, broke out in 1798 and continued for two years. While French and American vessels fought at sea, Adams pressured Congress into passing the Alien and Sedition

Acts, some of the most repressive pieces of legislation in American history, which effectively criminalized dissent at the executive's discretion. The Quasi-War came to an end when both sides realized they were gaining little and losing much from their spat.

In September 1796, in the midst of these conflicts on the high seas, first with Britain and then with France, President Washington published his *Farewell Address*, and with it unveiled one of the most fundamental and enduring visions of America's role in the world. The *Address* said much about the rightful place of religion and virtue in a democracy, as well as the unexpected rise of political parties, but its most important contribution was a clear statement of American unilateralism. The United States, Washington pronounced, "must steer clear of permanent alliances with any portion of the foreign world." The ongoing backdrop of hostility with Britain and France provided an obvious justification for such a unilateral policy, but Washington worried as much about the deleterious effect foreign affairs was having on America's domestic tranquility and political stability. The best policy, then, was neutrality.

Contrary to national myth, however, Washington's *Farewell Address* was not a statement of "isolationism." People of the late eighteenth century inhabited a thoroughly interconnected— indeed globalized—world, and pure isolation would have been impossible for the American government and financially ruinous for the American people. Washington never entertained the fantasy of isolation, and the term "isolationism" was still unknown during his time. Instead, he advocated that the United States enter into commercial arrangements with all and, when necessary, temporary political or military alliances with some, to ensure the military and economic security—and, not least of all, the domestic political harmony—of the United States. This canonical proclamation of supposed "isolationism" called for thoroughgoing international commercial and cultural relations, and recognized the deep international involvement such a position would require of the United States. Jefferson, who became president in 1801, reiterated Washington's message of unilateralism—that is, active international engagement on America's own terms—when he called for "peace, commerce, and honest friendship with all nations, entangling alliances with none" in his inaugural address.

A second war for independence

For forty years, American relations with Britain and France whipsawed between conflict and cooperation. Not coincidentally, these four decades marked the age of revolution, with contention between Britain and France at the very heart of revolutionary violence and Americans, busy advancing their own agenda, usually trapped somewhere in the middle. But with the end of the Quasi-War in 1800, and tensions with the British settled by the Jay Treaty, Americans entering the Jeffersonian era would have been excused for thinking that their international troubles were behind them.

Peace lasted only a few years, and when fighting resumed in Europe it was only a matter of time before the United States would be dragged in yet again. The British reprised their role as the pantomime villain opposed to American virtue, both at sea and along the western borderlands. From 1805, the Royal Navy once again seized American ships and their goods; they also began seizing men, on the grounds that many of them were still subjects of the king, and forcing them into service. This policy of impressment provoked a furious reaction in the United States. The most notorious incident occurred in 1807, when the British warship HMS *Leopard* bombarded a US Navy ship, the USS *Chesapeake*, off the Virginia coast, boarded it, and impressed four American sailors, one of whom was hanged for desertion from the Royal Navy. Britain declared that any neutral vessel wishing to trade with continental Europe, now completely dominated by France, first had to call at a port in the British Isles for inspection and clearance, threatening American profit as well as pride.

American anger was further stoked by British provocations in the west, as the British once again encouraged American Indian nations to resist America's westward expansion.

Jefferson was caught in a bind familiar to several American presidents from Washington to Wilson: to accede to Europe's demands was tantamount to accepting international vassal status, but to resist was tantamount to an act of war against the hegemonic power in the Atlantic world. Refusing to ally with European states, even fellow neutrals, that were also resisting the British blockade, Jefferson instead opted for a disastrous middle ground: an economic embargo of all US trade with Britain that was virtually unenforceable and widely ignored.

Designed to forestall war, Jefferson's middling strategy in fact made it all but inevitable, particularly when he was succeeded as president in 1809 by James Madison, a brilliant political theorist but inept politician. Urged on by "war hawks," mostly from the South and West who wanted westward expansion, Congress declared war in the summer of 1812. Despite inflicting a good deal of destruction, neither side could build any momentum in the conflict that followed, and ultimately neither side secured its key war aims. An American invasion of Canada saw the burning of York (now Toronto) and naval battles on the Great Lakes. A British drive into upstate New York failed, and while another incursion into Maryland initially succeeded—resulting in the sack of Washington, DC, and the burning of the presidential mansion— it too was eventually turned back.

On Christmas Eve in 1814, British and American negotiators in the Flemish town of Ghent agreed to peace terms that lacked much definition or resolution but allowed both sides to stop fighting and save face. The War of 1812 ended as it began, in a stalemate with neither side having made any real gains. This was enough for the Americans, however, who celebrated as if it were a great victory. And it some sense, it was: the experimental republic,

1. This print, made in London, depicts the British attack on Washington, DC, in August 1814. Although the war was a stalemate, Americans celebrated it as a second war of independence.

a squabbling federation spread thinly over thousands of miles of territory, had for the second time fended off one of the most powerful empires in world history. Despite a secessionist threat from New England, which had angrily objected to the war (on grounds of self-interest rather than outright pacifism), nationalism surged throughout the United States. The British presence in North America receded somewhat after the war, threats to US security diminished and then disappeared, and a new sense of national cohesion took hold. For these reasons, the War of 1812 has been dubbed "the second war of independence."

America first

Conditions were now perfect for the unilateral nation to flourish. American statesmen heeded Washington and Jefferson and avoided permanent, entangling alliances, leaving them free to act

attitude has been the

in the world as they pleased. There were some constraints on US behavior, but not many.

In 1823, in a doctrine that would bear his name in perpetuity, President James Monroe formalized this prevailing doctrine of unilateralism. Like all presidential doctrines that followed, general theory emerged directly out of particular circumstance—the president used an immediate crisis to justify existing policy and put forth ground rules for future conduct. In the early 1820s, Latin America was embroiled in a series of nationalist revolutions, which people in the United States feared could lead to another European power, such as France or Russia, taking over Spain's crumbling empire. Simultaneously, a group of powerful Americans began pressing for intervention against the Ottomans in the Greek Civil War, a risky venture with few US national interests at stake.

The Monroe Doctrine, which was for the most part actually drafted by Secretary of State John Quincy Adams, solved this geopolitical dilemma. It declared to the European powers that the Western Hemisphere was geographically separate and politically distinct, and that therefore Europe shouldn't meddle in inter-American affairs. In exchange, Monroe promised that the United States would refrain from inserting itself into European issues. The Monroe Doctrine promised that America wouldn't interfere with Europe's existing New World colonies, but it did lay down further rules: non-transferability, which meant that colonial sovereignty couldn't be transferred from one European empire to another and that the end of a power's colonial rule must lead to national independence for that colony; and non-expansion, which meant that European empires couldn't extend their domain in the Americas.

The Monroe Doctrine was also unapologetically unilateralist in its execution: the British, happy with building a more informal, economic empire in South America and confident that they could hold on to their existing formal colonies, held similar fears that Spain's colonies would fall into French or Russian hands. Knowing that they now both viewed the international situation in similar terms, London had initially approached the Monroe administration with an offer of a partnership. Several members of the Monroe cabinet wanted to accept the British offer, but Adams insisted that the United States go it alone.

The combined effect of the War of 1812 and the Monroe Doctrine was monumental: the first principles of international unilateralism and moral exceptionalism were now so firmly entrenched that they became the lodestars for the United States in the world. Americans believed, now more than ever, that the United States was a chosen nation, different and better than others and destined for great things. As such, it had a mandate to act on its own, unsullied and unrestricted by partnerships with other states. In the following decades, these traits—a sense of destiny and an avoidance of allies—propelled the relentless expansion of the United States westward.

-Take it /farm it /exploit it

Chapter 2
Expansionism

> *most educated/literate!*
> *wealthies*

For nearly three hundred years, the people who inhabited what came to be called the United States enlarged their territorial holdings. From their original base that ranged from New England to the Carolinas, Americans pushed their boundaries westward and southward until the United States was the sovereign power from the Atlantic to the Pacific and the Rio Grande to the Great Lakes. As they did so, their belief that expansion wasn't just inevitable but righteous took hold: progress was good, and the United States represented progress; therefore, many started believing that the best thing for all concerned was to stretch US borders as far as possible. To some extent this expansionism, which was not simply a process of settlement but an ideology of rightful conquest, defined the American national character as much as anything else.

> *progress = ideology of rightful conquest*

Expansionism was not a new phenomenon; it simply expressed old ideas more powerfully than ever before. Development, especially but not solely economic in nature, has been frenetic and relentless—and above all constant—throughout American history. More important than that, though, has been a consistent *belief* in development, akin to a secular faith that expansion will lead to a happier and more prosperous future. "We have no interest in the scenes of antiquity," the nation's foremost champion of expansion, John L. O'Sullivan, claimed in 1839. "The expansive future is our arena, and for our history." The United States, he concluded, was unique because it was "the great nation of futurity." →

This faith in the future, more specifically in Americans' own capacity to bend the future to their will, has been powerful enough to withstand the profoundly destabilizing results of expansionism, especially war. The period between the War of 1812 and the Civil War, commonly remembered as the Jacksonian era but perhaps more appropriately called "the age of O'Sullivan," unleashed these restless impulses and their violent effects across a continent, and set the ideological template for even greater expansions to follow.

European decent

An extensive sphere

American Foreign Relations

The people behind American expansionism were not originally from the North American continent. Their European ancestors had moved to the land that would become America in flight from persecution, in search of economic betterment, or both. Until midway through the antebellum period, these European residents for the most part hailed from (or descended from those who hailed from) England, Scotland, Wales, and Ulster, though other Protestant refugees—including Dutch, Swedes, Germans, and French Huguenots—as well as small pockets of Catholics and Jews could be found up and down the east coast of North America. Because they weren't the land's original inhabitants, their expansionist drives occurred at the expense of those who were known for most of American history as Indians and more recently as Native Americans or American Indians. The transplantation of the other large group of overseas migrants—that is, African slaves—was also critical to American expansion, even if the slaves themselves were unwilling expansionists.

Displacing the continent's original inhabitants, sometimes through treaties but more often at gunpoint, upset some Americans, but most saw it as an unpleasant means to a highly desirable end. Racism played a large role in justifying expansion:

↳ common reason

with an economy fueled in large part by slavery (increasingly so after 1800) and the expulsion of American Indians from their ancestral lands, successive generations of Americans founded a nation on the idea of white superiority. Such racism was backed by legal norms, religious dogma, and a firm belief in an ideal of civilization. White settlers from England, for example, held fast to a legal doctrine based on the proper use of land: if it was unclaimed and unsettled, and left to lie fallow, it was considered unowned and available for the taking. When they arrived in North America in the seventeenth and eighteenth centuries, these settlers had little sense of how nomadic Indians used their land, but they could see that it hadn't been developed for villages, towns, or pastureland familiar to European eyes. Even when American Indians had settled an area, it hadn't been done in a way befitting European customs—meaning it hadn't been effectively settled at all.

Yet all of these notions—law, religion, and civilization—also instilled in Americans a sense of obligation to the supposedly benighted peoples who lacked a legal code, the Christian faith, and modern standards of civility. As they spread their territorial sovereignty, Americans felt they also had a duty to spread their values. They were more powerful than their aboriginal neighbors, and this disparity of economic and military power helped germinate a reformist impulse in the British colonies that became especially pronounced once the United States was founded and cast its gaze westward. By the turn of the nineteenth century, the ideology of expansionism was therefore grounded not only in the right of conquest, but also in the responsibility to improve the lives of others—which of course further deepened the American confidence that expansion was just and noble. Whether reformism was a sincerely held belief or mere cover for perennial land grabs, two powerful impulses—selfless ideals and selfish interests— coexisted without irony or conflict in the American worldview and provided a potent ideology for guiding America in the world for centuries to come.

Thus when the United States was created in the years from 1775 to 1783, expansionism was already on the minds of its people. After all, the origins of the American Revolution lay in the hated Proclamation Line of 1763, which barred colonial settlement beyond the Appalachians. Tellingly, the only time Congress passed effective legislation under the ineffectual Articles of Confederation came in 1787, with the passage of the Northwest Ordinance. As a large-scale survey and organization of territory Britain had ceded in 1783, the Ordinance was a triumph of basic land planning. It also established a vital principle for future American expansion: new lands acquired by the United States (a widely shared expectation) would be incorporated as territories under federal government jurisdiction; when enough people had moved into the territory, and settled and developed it to a sufficient extent, the territory could apply for statehood as a full member of the Union. In the ensuing decades, this vast stretch of land, known as the Indiana Territory, was subdivided into the states of Ohio, Indiana, Illinois, Michigan, and Wisconsin.

The United States now had an orderly, legal system for perpetual expansion. In fact, the Ordinance established a framework for a new kind of state—not really a nation-state at all, but something more like an empire-state. The original thirteen colonies were the metropole: they provided the engine of economic growth, the capital and technological expertise needed to consolidate new land holdings, and a steady supply of willing migrants. This empire differed in that its colonies (i.e., territories, such as the Indiana Territory created from the Northwest Ordinance) were not ruled as subservient components, but as impending equal partners in a federal state.

As an exercise in nation-building, it is difficult to exaggerate the influence of the Northwest Ordinance. As a declaration of intent, it staked about as firm a land claim as possible—no longer would there be any ambiguity about who was intending to settle the Northwest. Even more, the principle of expansive settlement, already axiomatic in the American imagination, had been codified in law. According to the French Enlightenment philosopher Montesquieu, republics had to be small in order to survive; the larger they became, the more disputatious and divisive their people became, making effective government all but impossible. But James Madison, the most sophisticated political theorist among the Founders, turned Montesquieu's dictum on its head: factions were inevitable, and so to accommodate them and give them room to express themselves, the American republic had to grow in order to flourish. "This form of government, in order to effect its purposes, must operate not within a small but an extensive sphere," he told his fellow Virginian Thomas Jefferson in 1787.

With the promise of seemingly endless territory available to the west, and with an ideological justification in hand, American statesmen wasted little time in proclaiming a brighter future for a grander United States. "However our present interests may restrain us within our own limits," Jefferson wrote to James Monroe, then the governor of Virginia, in 1801, "it is impossible not to look forward to distant times, when our rapid multiplication will expand itself beyond those limits, and cover the whole northern, if not the southern continent, with a people speaking the same language, governed in similar forms, and by similar laws." John Quincy Adams, after Jefferson probably the most important architect of expansionism, was only slightly less ambitious. The United States, he predicted to his wife Louisa on the eve of the War of 1812, was to be "coextensive with the North American continent, destined by God and nature to be the most populous and most powerful people ever combined under one social compact."

Manifest Destiny

The problem, of course, was that the land Jefferson and Adams wanted as their own was still occupied by a variety of American

Indian nations backed, unofficially, by Great Britain and Spain. Expansion was therefore unlikely to be peaceful. Jefferson's letter to Monroe predicted a glorious future, but he ended on an ominous note: "Nor can we contemplate with satisfaction either blot or mixture on that surface." This did not bode well for the people who were in the path of American expansion—that is, those who already lived on the coveted land and represented potential blots on the map and sources of unhealthy racial mixing. With Southern slavery about to enter its boom years, thanks to the invention of the cotton gin, and propel American settlement further south and west, the new republic was poised to advance on a platform of racial supremacy. With this dark twist to the exceptionalist vision, the displacement of others who stood in the way of American expansion became easier to justify.

American expansionism embodied the phenomenon of "settler colonialism," the most unstoppable form of conquest because it relentlessly focused on only one thing: the control of land. Settler colonialism had no room for the sharing of power or sovereignty— the people who initially lived on the land weren't asked to collaborate or swear allegiance, but simply to leave and never return. Liberal imperialism, the theory on which settler colonialism rested, was supposed to be enlightened as it promoted democratic values while also appreciating the diversity of other cultures. But because it was based on concepts like private property, individual rights, and economic development, its effects were irreversible. The expansion of liberalism, in other words, rested on highly illiberal methods.

George Washington understood the problem well. His military career had begun as an officer in the colonial militia in the 1750s, when he was charged with clearing a path for English settlement in the Ohio Valley. In 1754, a clash he instigated with the French turned out to be the opening battle of the French and Indian War, and by extension the Seven Years' War. But at the same time, Washington was also an investor in the Ohio Company, one of the most important colonial ventures in westward expansion and whose clients Washington, then a major in the British Army, had been assigned to protect in 1754. Therefore, he also grasped the significance of settler colonialism from the ground up. Washington's strategy was to give diplomacy a try, but settle America's land west of the Mississippi by force if necessary. Secretary of War Henry Knox, one of Washington's closest advisers, shared this ambivalence. Knox hoped that American Indian tribes could become civilized and integrated into the American body politic, and he had a subtle appreciation of their qualities as well as disdain for the violent unruliness of American settlers. He also realized that the future would be dictated by the needs and desires of the United States. "This is the last offer that can be made," Knox bluntly told the tribes of the Northwest. "If you do not embrace it now, your doom must be sealed forever."

As the American Indians well knew, the problem with diplomacy was that it was simply a way to clear the land for American settlement and development. Any treaty an Indian nation signed was a capitulation, a suicide note for an entire way of life, even if they agreed to peace terms and integration within the United States. Faced with such a choice, and encouraged by the British, they opted for war.

Low-intensity warfare, punctuated by vicious but conclusive battles, would define the territory covered by the Northwest Ordinance from 1790 to the end of the War of 1812. Indians and Americans saw their fortunes wax and wane, but the general pattern saw Indians suffer the bulk of defeats and Americans score most of the victories, and by the end of the War of 1812 there was no longer any doubt that the land north of the Ohio and east of the Mississippi rivers belonged exclusively to the United States. The Americans notched their first major victory in 1794, at the Battle of Fallen Timbers near the shores of Lake Erie. The decisive turning point came in 1811, with William Henry Harrison's famous victory over Tecumseh at the Battle of Tippecanoe in present-day Indiana. The War of 1812, a stalemate for Britain and the United States but a disaster for Native Americans, meant that Indian settlement east of the Mississippi and north of the Ohio was no longer tenable.

By then, thanks to Jefferson, the principle of perpetual expansion had become enshrined as an aspect of national identity. In 1803, he acquired the Louisiana Territory, by purchase rather than conquest, from France. At the time, this tract of land was considerably larger than present-day Louisiana—the Territory covered nearly a million square miles of land between the Mississippi River and the Rocky Mountains that stretched, after skirting the boundary with Spanish Tejas (Texas), from New Orleans on the Gulf of Mexico to the eventual border with Canada.

expansion of all-country

By 1815, the United States had laid claim to two-thirds of what would become the continental United States. The acquisition of Louisiana gave the United States the right to conquer and settle the territory free of European influence, but doing so meant dealing with the hundreds of Indian tribes living on it, a process which unfolded over decades, both peacefully and violently. Beyond Louisiana, expansionists such as Adams maneuvered to secure everything else and make the republic a transcontinental nation-state.

Spanish Florida was the first target. General Andrew Jackson, hero of the War of 1812, initiated the process by invading Florida in 1818, ostensibly to quell Spanish and Indian harassment of settlers in the state of Georgia and the Alabama Territory (in truth, it was American settlers who were encroaching on Spanish and Indian lands). Jackson routed what opposition there was and presented Secretary of State Adams with an opportunity to enlarge the Union yet again. Though Jackson had exceeded his instructions and invaded Florida on his own accord, Adams gratefully accepted his gift—and went further still. In negotiations

↳ past the appalachains

32

with Spain, Adams insisted not merely on the cession of all of Florida but also on Spanish recognition that the legal southern border of the United States stretched all the way to the Pacific. With the signing of the Transcontinental Treaty in 1819, Adams went a long way to realizing the prophecy he had made to his wife eight years before.

After becoming president in 1829, Jackson furthered the expansionist project, again with violence. Unlike their fellow tribes to the north, the American Indians of the non-Louisiana south had managed to arrange, by treaty, a recognition of permanent settlement in the United States. Even more, in 1832 the Supreme Court upheld the Indians' status as sovereign states within the United States. But while the Cherokee, Chickasaw, Choctaw, and Creek had a legal right to remain where they were, they were also obstacles to white settlement and the expansion of slavery in the states of Georgia, Tennessee, Alabama, Mississippi, and both Carolinas. Ignoring the Supreme Court's ruling, Jackson ordered federal troops to remove the Indian nations to a territory west of the Mississippi River later known as Oklahoma.

Although Indian removal did not lead to any further territorial gains, it was critical to American expansionism as both a moment of consolidation and a spur to further growth. Over the next decade, the United States poured across the North American continent like water moving downhill, diverting only when an obstacle blocked its path. Earlier, in the War of 1812, that obstacle had been British and Canadian resolve. British power also served as a check on American designs for territory beyond the land acquired in the Louisiana Purchase. Later, it was Americans' own ideological and political reservations that put a brake to expansion. Slavery was the most pressing of these divisive issues, but there were others too. Following the Mexican War, for example, it was US reluctance to absorb Spanish-speaking, Catholic Mexicans who lived south of the Rio Grande. Aside from their own inhibitions, then, by the 1840s the only thing that could

going west

2. John Gast's 1872 painting, "American Progress," presents manifest destiny as a civilizing force, with white settlers, farmers, and miners driving American Indians and wild animals from the land. The idealized woman represents progress—she's carrying a schoolbook, leading the railroads, and laying telegraph wire behind her.

put a limit on the continental expansion of the United States was the Pacific Ocean.

Expansionism had long been part of the fabric of American exceptionalism, and vice versa, but the link between expansion and nationalism had never been as fully and as explicitly developed as in the antebellum era—and nobody did as much to make it happen as John L. O'Sullivan. A journalist and Democratic Party activist based in New York, O'Sullivan was also an ardent expansionist. For him, expansion was a divine calling, blending, to his mind, religious providentialism with Protestant notions of stewardship and Anglo-Saxon norms about the duty to cultivate arable land (or else forfeit title to it). It was, he wrote in a widely cited article from 1845, "the right of our manifest destiny to overspread and to possess the whole of

34

the continent which Providence has given us for the development of the great experiment of liberty and federated self-government." With his newspaper, O'Sullivan popularized the new phrase, "manifest destiny," which in fact referred to a very old process. He argued that because of the lay of the land and its unique political and economic virtues, the United States had a right of conquest in North America. But, O'Sullivan and other expansionists went on to explain, the nation also had a responsibility to spread those very same political and economic virtues as it expanded westward. Territorial expansion couldn't simply occur for its own sake; it had to serve a larger purpose of civilizing a savage continent.

Most difficult aspects of expansion

A war of conquest

O'Sullivan was not writing in a vacuum. By 1845, Americans were eyeing expansion on three fronts: Texas, then an independent republic; California, then a province of Mexico; and the Oregon Country, a vast expanse of land stretching from the northern boundary of California to the southern tip of the Alaska Panhandle that was also partly claimed by Britain.

Ten years before, after absorbing wave upon wave of Anglo settlers from the United States, Texas had fought a brief war of independence and broke free from Mexico. The Anglo Texans petitioned to join the United States but were rebuffed. In 1820, the Missouri Compromise had established a principle of equality so that a new slave state had to be balanced with a new free state (in that case, Maine was created to balance out Missouri). In the intervening years, the controversy over slavery had greatly intensified, and Jackson, although a slave owner himself and no friend of abolitionism, felt he couldn't admit a large slave state such as Texas without balancing it with a non-slave state. Mexico, still nursing its wounded national pride from the Texan conflict, had also made it clear that annexation of the Texan region to the United States would be construed as an act of war.

By 1845, a parallel standoff over the fate of Oregon was also coming to a head. Claimed by both London and Washington, the Oregon Country possessed enormous economic potential. For expansionists like Adams, it would provide the United States with its foreordained Pacific outlet and consummate the vision he had expressed in the Transcontinental Treaty. But like the Mexicans, the British threatened war if the United States tried to seize all of Oregon.

Despite being an integral part of Mexico (a fellow revolutionary republic and postcolonial nation-state in the New World), California was also in American sights. This was perhaps the most desirable of all territories, but it was also the least accessible: Texas was independent and was actively petitioning to join the United States, while Britain acknowledged an American claim to at least part of Oregon. Those would be difficult acquisitions, but acquiring California would be an act of outright conquest.

Events didn't unfold as neatly as it seems on paper, 170 years later, but the standoff ended in 1845–46 with a series of quick developments that broke almost completely in America's favor. This was no surprise, for the United States was in a dominant position. First, Texas joined the United States in 1845. The next year, with a Mexican war brewing, President James K. Polk, a devout expansionist, agreed to split Oregon almost equally with Britain at the 49th parallel. That freed Polk to complete the expansionist agenda in California. After American troops provoked an incident along the disputed border that served as a pretext for reprisal, Congress declared war against Mexico in May 1846; fighting culminated with the US Army's capture of Mexico City in September 1847. The peace treaty, signed the following February, forced Mexico to relinquish its northern provinces (territory that became the states of California, Arizona, Utah, Nevada, and New Mexico, in addition to parts of several others) and recognize US sovereignty over Texas in exchange for an indemnity of $15 million. Five years later, in 1853, the Gadsden

Purchase acquired a narrow strip of land in southern Arizona, thus completing the incorporation of the continental United States. Territorial expansion of the United States on the North American continent finished with the Alaska Purchase of 1867.

While spectacularly successful in terms of the territorial expansion and military glory it attained, the Mexican War rested on a set of dubious moral foundations. The first was that territorial gains in the southwest, from Texas westward, raised the specter of the expansion of slavery, which exacerbated strife between Southern slavery apologists and Northern abolitionists and free-soil advocates which, in turn, triggered an escalation of tensions that erupted in the secession crisis of 1860–61. Indeed, it's no exaggeration to say that the Mexican War was the opening battle of the Civil War. The Mexican War's second, equally dubious foundation was its very reason for being: land. The unprompted assault on Mexico was clearly a land grab. Finally, the war's proximate cause, a Mexican incursion onto American soil, was contested at the time and has been derided ever since. Not wanting to be seen as a conqueror, and with tensions along the disputed borderlands running high after the US annexation of Texas, Polk waited for an advantageous moment to strike. Mexican culpability was doubtful even when the moment came, leading a freshman Congressman from Illinois, Abraham Lincoln, to introduce his famous "Spot Resolutions" demanding that Polk come clean about the exact location of the clash between US and Mexican troops.

Unsurprisingly, then, the war caused deep divisions within American society that were partly regional and partisan. In the process, war with Mexico crystallized what would become an increasingly salient feature of American foreign relations: the antiwar movement. On the whole, Democrats were unabashed expansionists, but many Whigs were uneasy about a war for expansion that was also, at least in spirit, a war for slavery. The Revolutionary War and the War of 1812 had galvanized antiwar opposition too, but on both occasions dissent was stimulated by the fact that some—for instance, Loyalists to the British crown in the 1770s or New England merchants in 1814—had something to lose. In other words, dissent before 1846 wasn't so much a principled stand about the morality of war, but rather a fear of the material effects a particular war would have. The Mexican War was different. While it didn't spawn a mass movement, it did trigger widespread opposition based on a sense that what the federal government was doing was immoral. Part of the opposition to the war with Mexico was purely pacifist; the nineteenth century marked the emergence of a peace movement that condemned war under any circumstances. But some Americans, such as Congressman Lincoln, opposed the war because they thought their nation was in the wrong.

Such antiwar passion did little to deter Polk, but it did have some influence because, ironically, it infused American war and diplomacy with a special moral fervor and sense of mission. Exceptionalism did not always pull Americans in the same direction: it could lead a patriot into a war for national glory, but it could also lead a patriot to conclude that his or her beloved nation had gone astray. Antiwar activism in the United States has rarely been anti-American; that is, it has rarely been a critique of the United States itself, instead focusing on the misguided or corrupt elites who were betraying America's true ideals. So when critics of a particular war—in this case, Lincoln of Polk in Mexico—raised an equally exceptionalist critique of the war's purposes and objectives, it forced presidents and other wartime leaders to justify their actions as pursuant to the most noble goals worthy of America and its values. Held to account by crusaders for peace, the architects of war claimed that they fought wars of civilization and progress, not glory and conquest. Expansion was pursued for the good of humanity, not simply the United States. Designed to stop war, antiwar idealism simply pushed the United States to portray its wars as moral crusades.

Rebirth of a nation

No crusade proved grander than the Civil War, which began as a war for national union but also became the nation's first war of humanitarian intervention. Two moral causes, nationalism and emancipation, infused a sense of destiny among pro-Union Americans. Theirs was to be a war of redemption—not just for the United States, but for the world at large. Ever since the signing of the Declaration of Independence, Americans had seen their nation as the repository for humanity's dreams and ambitions. The United States was not simply a nation-state but a moral project, bound by natural law and divine providence to spread its enlightened systems of self-government and individual opportunity as widely as possible. Thus at its gravest moment of peril, when slave-owning aristocrats in the South moved to break up the United States, Lincoln led the North in a furious, righteous crusade. "We say we are for the Union. The world will not forget that we say this," Lincoln said to Congress in 1862. "We shall nobly save or meanly lose the last best hope of earth." America's struggle was also the world's, and with it would go the fate of other nations' hopes for freedom.

Bloody as it was, the Civil War ended well for the Union. After an uneven start, Lincoln and his generals found a winning formula by 1864 and ground the Confederate armies into submission in a nasty, sanguinary war of attrition. Through skillful diplomacy, Secretary of State William Seward managed to keep Britain and France at bay—both relied to some extent on Southern cotton, and both would have been happy to see the United States, a continental power of awesome but troublesome potential, broken in two—and the war came to an end in April 1865.

In the context of global developments, the American Civil War wasn't unique—in fact, it wasn't even unusual. The Industrial Revolution that began in Britain in the late eighteenth century and spread elsewhere had, by the middle of the nineteenth century, stimulated two important phenomena: the growth of the state and the surge of nationalism. On one hand, the pressures of modern industrial economies led to the centralization of state power, and with it the growth of elaborate governing structures, such as bureaucracies, to manage the increasingly complicated and intricate workings of state and society. On the other, the revolutions of the 1770s and '80s and the rise of an industrial workforce prompted mass movements of people. One result of this was the spread of democracy; another was the rise of nationalism. These two processes—the growth and modernization of the state, and the advent of popular nationalism—often catalyzed each other to produce warfare. This was because as nations formed, or were re-formed, the very purposes and values of the nation-state—the political culture that would bind its people together in a national union—were up for grabs.

The American Civil War was very much an episode in this broader global development. Between 1861 and 1871, the imperative to modernize led several other nation-states to invent or utterly transform themselves, including Germany, Italy, Russia, Japan, and Canada. There was, however, one key difference with the United States: scale. The enormity of the American modernization project overshadowed them all, with profound consequences for US engagement with the wider world ever since.

Thus it's entirely fitting that the Civil War also initiated a major push to settle the American West and consolidate an entire continent under the banner of a single nation-state. The Civil War enforced US sovereignty in the South, but, with Southerners no longer in Congress to complicate expansionism, it also provided an opportunity to do so in the West. With the expansion of slavery no longer at issue, Congress duly passed the Homestead Act in 1862, which organized the giving away of millions of acres of federal territory beyond the Mississippi; the aim was to encourage white Americans to migrate westward and settle the land. They first needed to get there, and then once there, to interact with the rest of the nation, so the following year saw construction begin on the Transcontinental Railroad that would connect California to the Midwest and, by extension, markets in the East.

Yet once again, Americans were not moving into empty, virgin land. By instigating the final installment of America's long-running Indian Wars, the Civil War's westward push proved to be as violent as its campaigns in the South. A series of interlocking conflicts stretching over nearly four decades began in 1857 with the Utah War, followed by the Dakota War in Minnesota (1862), the Colorado War (1863–65), the Black Hawk War in Utah (1865–72), Red Cloud's War in Montana and Wyoming (1866–68), and the Great Sioux War in Montana and South Dakota (1876–77), famed for the Battle of Little Bighorn. With the exception of General George Custer's humiliation at Little Bighorn, these wars produced one lopsided victory after another for the United States and the near-destruction and forced removal of American Indian tribes; the most infamous incident was probably the Sand Creek Massacre of November 1864 (in present-day Colorado, near the Kansas border), but such atrocities were not unusual. Other, smaller battles raged throughout the West as settler colonialism was unleashed across the continent, with Americans farming, mining, and foresting, and railroad companies began binding the nation ever more tightly together. The American Indian Wars began drawing to a close with the Dawes Act of 1887, which set forth a program for the regulation of Indians' affairs and their eventual assimilation. The last major fighting occurred in the Ghost Dance War in South Dakota, in 1890–91, notorious for the massacre at Wounded Knee.

These parallel conflicts for national consolidation and integration, against the Confederacy in the South and American Indians in the West, provided the United States with a platform for its next, most ambitious round of expansionism yet: global power.

Chapter 3
Global America

By the end of the nineteenth century, the United States had become the world's preeminent economic power. Its industrial output had eclipsed that of its European rivals—indeed, that of nearly all of Europe combined—and its financial sector would soon surpass Great Britain's. The continental United States, integrated by an extensive network of railroads and telegraph wires, was a vast but cohesive internal market that provided for nearly all of the nation's economic needs: natural resources and arable land were plentiful, numerous ports on two oceans and the Gulf of Mexico provided key links to overseas markets, and access to capital from American banks was relatively open. Imports flowed in and exports flowed out, but in essence the country was economically self-sufficient.

Yet for such a large and wealthy country, by 1890 the United States was in a curious position: it was an economic colossus, but a diplomatic and military dwarf. In comparison to the great powers of Europe, or Japan, Americans were minor actors on the world stage. Outside the Western Hemisphere, the United States had little influence in global affairs. That would all soon change.

Of course, Americans had never been reluctant to stray beyond their own borders. When circumstances warranted, they were more than willing to engage the outside world, including political involvement and military intervention. And it wasn't as if the American presence in the world was minimal. Thousands of merchants, missionaries, and other itinerants traveled, lived abroad, and served as unofficial ambassadors of the United States to the rest of the world. Even more important was the flow of immigrants into the United States, a tide that reached epic proportions around the turn of the century. Many of these immigrants remained for good in their new home, but a sizable number either returned to their country of origin or kept traversing back and forth. These millions of people, whether inbound or outbound, served as bridges linking America to the world.

The process we now call globalization accelerated in the last decades of the nineteenth century. International flows of goods, people, ideas, and capital increased in frequency, intensity, and reach, and the world became ever more interconnected. The United States was not at the center of globalization—that position was held by the British Empire, with the Royal Navy, the City of London, and the great manufacturing centers of the midlands and the north as its engines—but it was very much an integral part of the worldwide connections being forged in the period between the Civil War and World War I.

By 1900, the world was thoroughly interconnected, thanks to technological innovation, but it was also becoming more interdependent—that is, what happened in one region affected what happened in another region, even if those two regions had had little previous contact. To use an example that particularly frustrated American officials, when Czarist Russia tolerated anti-Jewish pogroms in its countryside, Russian Jews fled en masse to the United States, as it was the only country that could offer them both easy employment and a safe haven. As a result, Americans had a much greater awareness of their role as citizens of the world. As the missionary leader Josiah Strong put it, globalization had made "the whole world a neighborhood and every man a neighbor."

1898 and all that

Still, informal, transnational ties between people weren't the same thing as the projection of international power, and until the last years of the nineteenth century, US foreign policy was a rather sedate affair. The American military was unusually small for an emerging power, especially one with such a large population and economy, and the American foreign service was amateurish and understaffed. The reason for such neglect of the levers of international power was simple: until the 1890s, the need for US political and military involvement in Europe and Asia was hardly self-evident, the requirements for continental self-defense were minimal, and economically the domestic market was huge, and thus sufficient.

That easy complacence disappeared suddenly thanks to an ongoing crisis in the Spanish colony of Cuba—ironically, a controversy on America's doorstep created the conditions for it to become a global power of genuine importance. The cause of Cuban independence—*Cuba Libre*—erupted in the early 1890s when Spain was at a particularly low point, yet desperate to retain one of its last imperial treasures. Fighting broke out in the winter of 1895. Cuban insurgents made initial gains, but they faced a brutal Spanish counteroffensive that included the forcible rounding up of non-combatants and cordoning them in internment camps, or *concentrados* (the first use of modern concentration camps). In the United States, the outcry at this humanitarian disaster was emotional and shrill, partly because such atrocities seemed new (though they weren't—the US Army had resorted to similarly brutal tactics in the American Indian Wars), and partly because the Cuban rebels, many of them exiles living in New York, had launched a savvy public relations campaign to win American support. American newspapers, especially New York's infamous "yellow press," were all too happy to sensationalize Spanish atrocities. By 1898, Americans were increasingly supportive of intervening directly in the Cuban war of independence.

3. The war with Spain in Cuba was the first overseas conflict in which American intervention was seen as principally humanitarian. In this drawing from the New York magazine *Puck*, pointedly titled "Then and Now," the atrocities committed by Spanish soldiers are contrasted with the benevolence of the United States.

President William McKinley, a Civil War veteran who had seen enough bloodshed in his time, was reluctant to intervene in Cuba, but with public anger at the Spanish running so high he felt he had little choice. In January 1898, he deployed a US warship, the *Maine*, to Havana harbor to monitor the worsening situation onshore. A few weeks later, the ship exploded while at anchor. The yellow press and members of Congress blamed the Spanish, though it was likely the result of an accidental fire in the ship's hold. McKinley was still reluctant, but he could resist for only so long. As Kristin Hoganson has shown, insecurities about masculinity ran high in this era, and public officials worried about looking weak and "unmanly." Congress declared war against Spain in April 1898.

Fighting broke out soon after. The US Navy blockaded ports in Cuba and Puerto Rico and shelled Spanish positions on the islands in May. American troops landed on Cuba in June and Puerto Rico in July and, aided substantially by Cuban anti-colonial fighters, had effective control of both islands within weeks. Within three months of war being declared, Spain had been completely wiped out as an imperial power in the Western Hemisphere. But the war had another key theater as well, in the Pacific, where Spain still held colonial possessions. Soon after declaring war, US ships sailed from their makeshift Pacific headquarters in Hong Kong to Manila and routed the Spanish fleet. The US Navy brought with it Emilio Aguinaldo, the exiled leader of the anti-Spanish Filipino independence movement, who entered Manila, rallied his forces, and proclaimed Filipino independence. Aguinaldo's troops defeated the Spanish in a series of battles in June and July, and in August American soldiers invaded the capital of the Philippines, Manila.

For good reason, Secretary of State John Hay called it "a splendid little war"—for the United States, that is. In under a hundred days, the United States had routed a European colonial power in two different theaters spread across two transoceanic fronts. Overall American battle deaths were paltry—just under three hundred—and with the carnage of the Civil War still within living memory it convinced many that great-power status would come fairly easily. The Treaty of Paris, signed between Madrid and Washington in December, resulted in independence for Cuba and the transfer of sovereignty of the Philippines, Guam, and Puerto Rico to the United States; in return, Spain received $20 million.

The battles of 1898 demonstrated that the United States would become a global political and military power, and that its two most important regional spheres of influence, aside from the North American continent, would be the Caribbean and the Pacific. In this first age of globalization, the focus on maritime zones was not a coincidence. American strategists concentrated on the two critical seaward approaches to North America; if they could dominate those approaches, US security and prosperity would be assured, and American shipping, both commercial and naval, could easily penetrate Europe, Asia, and Africa.

Alfred Thayer Mahan, a Navy captain of undistinguished service but vast knowledge and intellect, provided the strategic rationale for this new departure. The truly great powers in history, Mahan argued, were strong at sea. Maritime power was also conducive to democracy, for it led states to build up their navies and merchant marines, which facilitated trade, rather than to maintain large standing armies, which were a potential source of authoritarian political power at home. With its security against foreign enemies assured, its long coastlines on two oceans and one of the world's great seas, and its republican political tradition, the United States was ideally suited to becoming a maritime power of enormous strength. American dominance of Cuba and the Philippines went a long way toward realizing Mahan's vision.

But the war of 1898 was hardly "splendid" for others. For the humiliated Spanish, of course, it was a total disaster, but its effects were not all that beneficial for some of the supposed victors either. For Cuban and Filipino freedom fighters, the war's outcome was at best bittersweet: their struggles for national independence had simply resulted in another form of colonial rule. This was formally the case for the Philippines, which was "annexed" by the United States, but it was effectively true for Cuba as well, which was independent but occupied and governed by the United States in all but name. As an expression of anti-colonial independence, *Cuba Libre* should have been retired in 1898. Instead, it became a rallying cry for future generations of Cubans, with adverse effects for everyone involved—Americans included.

With his goal of a truly self-governing Philippines in ruins, Aguinaldo and his forces began a new anti-colonial insurgency, but this time against his erstwhile ally, the United States. The Philippine-American War broke out in 1899, soon after it became clear that the Filipinos were not about to be granted independence. Aguinaldo was captured in 1901, and even though the insurgency continued without his leadership, it petered out the following year (though pockets of resistance endured for years).

Though mostly forgotten, the war in the Philippines was a critical watershed in US diplomatic history for three reasons. It was the first of many "small wars" of counterinsurgency that the US military would fight over the next century and more. In military technology, heavy weaponry, and naval power, Aguinaldo's forces were no match for the Americans. So they did what many ostensibly weaker forces do: play to their strengths, unassuming though they may be. Aguinaldo launched an insurgency that relied on surprise and mobility, not to mention support among the local populace. This prompted US forces to play to their strength: overwhelming firepower. The result was an eventual victory—or at least, the suppression of the anti-colonial resistance—but at the cost of over 4,000 US combat deaths and at least 250,000 Filipino lives, the majority of them civilians. The war was intensely controversial, partly because many Americans couldn't stomach a war for empire—their own country, after all, had been born in an anti-colonial rebellion—and partly because many were appalled by the brutal tactics American troops used in trying to suppress the insurgency. The most notorious was the so-called "water cure," which involved force-feeding water to a captured nationalist fighter until he talked or his stomach burst. Domestic opponents of the war formed the Anti-Imperialist League, organized protests and petitions, and held congressional hearings.

Second, this was America's first serious foray into Asia. Later, the United States fought three much larger wars against Japan and in Korea and Vietnam; later still came America's longest wars in Afghanistan and Iraq. These five wars have, each on their own but especially cumulatively, shaped not only America's military history but American history writ large. If America's "Asian century" has a point of origin, it was in the Philippines. In the war's wake, Hay issued the Open Door Notes of 1899 and 1900, which warned rival powers not to colonize China or close off its market to overseas trade. Keeping the door to East Asia open has remained a key American objective to this day.

Third, the Philippine War marked a key juncture in America's uneven record on promoting its ideals around the world. All strong states justify—often sincerely—the imposition of their power by invoking ideals, but few states have been as committed to spreading morals and values as the United States. For a long time, adhering to American values meant keeping apart from the rest of the world—not in isolation, of course, but by not mounting foreign crusades to convert others. The advent of globalization in the last few decades of the nineteenth century began to change the American worldview. It no longer seemed possible to separate the world into separate spheres of influence, as with the Monroe Doctrine. So if Americans were to become embedded in the world, they would do so by promoting their own values. What soon came to be called "national self-determination" was one of the most cherished of these ideals, and it helps to explain, in part, what attracted Americans to the anti-colonial cause of Cuban and Filipino nationalists in the first place. But the outcome of the war also revealed the limits of ideals when they directly clashed with national interests and racial prejudices. McKinley believed that Filipinos were incapable of self-government, and that if he didn't keep the Philippines then another great power—probably Germany but possibly Britain, France, or Japan—would seize the islands for itself. American Indians knew full well Americans' imperfect adherence to their promises of respecting the self-rule of others, but as the first of such instances of this dynamic overseas, the Cuban and Filipino cases marked a new departure in American statecraft. They would not, however, be the last.

America in the world war

The war kickstarted an increasingly activist world role for the United States. As globalization deepened, America's international portfolio widened. There were, to be sure, limits to the international impact on America. Uniquely among the great powers, it was self-sufficient economically, dependent upon neither imports for its foodstuffs and raw materials nor exports for its economic livelihood. But this didn't stop Americans from interjecting themselves into the world's political, military, cultural, and economic affairs more than ever before.

In 1858, the first transatlantic cable enabled the United States and Europe to communicate virtually instantaneously. In 1869, the Suez Canal linked the Mediterranean Sea with the Red Sea, enabling ships to pass relatively easily between the Atlantic and Indian oceans without going all the way around Africa. Between 1903 and 1914, America emulated this French achievement by constructing the Panama Canal, completing what was essentially an intercontinental, transoceanic waterway encircling the globe. Transcontinental railways spanning the United States (completed in 1869), Canada (1885), and Russia (1916) bound world travel and trade even tighter. Shipping and railroad links also enabled the expansion of agriculture, as farms found it possible to get their products to far-flung markets. The City of London, the world's financial hub before World War I, did much of the financing of these developments in the United States, but capital also flowed from Wall Street, as well as banks in Boston and San Francisco.

Americans not only helped shape globalization; they were deeply shaped by it as well. Most obviously, the unprecedented industrial boom of the late nineteenth and early twentieth centuries, known as the Machine Age, led to a surging demand for workers in American factories. Pushed by poverty and religious repression at home, approximately 20 million "new immigrants" migrated from southern and eastern Europe to the United States between the Civil War and World War I: "new" because they came from countries that hadn't before sent many immigrants to the United States and brought with them languages (Italian, Polish, Greek, Swedish, Norwegian, Russian, Yiddish, Chinese, Japanese, and others) and religions (Catholicism, Orthodox Christianity, Lutheranism, Orthodox Judaism, Buddhism, Confucianism) that had not had a significant presence in American society before.

4. Workers carve a path that would form the waterway of the Panama Canal. Conditions were brutal, and thousands died, but the canal was a significant engineering achievement that spurred globalization.

They maintained political ties with their countries of origin and expanded the remit of US foreign policy in the process.

Following the Open Door Notes, which established the principle of an international system based on openness, Americans were also playing a more active role in international war and diplomacy. In 1905, President Theodore Roosevelt brokered an end to the Russo-Japanese War. A student of Mahanian strategy, Roosevelt also embarked on an ambitious naval-building program that culminated in the circumnavigation of the American "great white fleet" in 1907–1908. His successor, William Howard Taft, continued these trends of combining maritime and commercial power in his "Dollar Diplomacy" policy, by which the US government partnered with private interests to influence development in other countries—for example, the building of railroads in China—that would also bring US foreign policy

51

greater international leverage. Though Dollar Diplomacy produced only mixed results in the short term, it signaled a way forward for American foreign policymakers to mobilize their nation's growing economic power.

By the eve of World War I in Europe, the United States had become an immensely powerful state. Its industrial economy exceeded all of Europe's and its financial resources were second only to Britain's. Its military, still small in the 1880s, was becoming more powerful, particularly its Navy; even more, it was evident that America's industrial and financial power would enable it to expand its military capabilities at will. In 1914, the United States was not the world's preeminent great power—Britain still held that distinction, followed closely by Germany and France, and possibly Russia and Japan—but it was one of the most powerful globally and was predominant in the Americas.

The outbreak of war in the summer of 1914 unexpectedly accelerated all these trends: the war brought about a collapse of Europe's power and created the conditions for the exponential growth of America's. From the trenches of Belgium and France, to the frontlines of northern Italy, to the grisly conditions of the eastern front between Germany and Russia, to the battles against Ottoman rule in Turkey and the Middle East, the war devastated Europe—physically, economically, and psychologically. The United States, by contrast, did very well. Trade with Europe, particularly the Allies of Britain and France, boomed, as nations at war desperately needed goods they couldn't produce themselves, certainly not at the Americans' low cost and high efficiency. With the war dragging on longer and costing much more than they had anticipated, Britain and France borrowed enormous amounts of money from American banks, and in 1916 New York eclipsed London as the hub of global finance.

The United States enjoyed this privileged position because it remained officially neutral when fighting broke out in 1914. President Woodrow Wilson was determined to keep the nation out of the war—Americans, he said, must be "neutral in fact, as well as in name" and "impartial in thought, as well as action"—and he was able to so until April 1917. This was actually not all that difficult. The only advocates for war were an influential but small contingent of elite Republicans, led by former president Theodore Roosevelt, while most Americans were opposed to intervention, among them the hierarchy of the Catholic Church, virtually all Protestant denominations, and millions of German-Americans and Irish-Americans, many of whom voted Democratic. In hindsight, an anti-German alliance with Britain and France seems normal, even natural, but in 1914 it was anything but. Indeed, the puzzle for historians isn't why it took so long for the United States to enter the war, but why the country ever did. *→ was not seen as necessary*

Wilson's appeal to neutrality was a fine sentiment, yet the result of American actions was hardly impartial: without design, the United States tilted in a pro-Allied direction. This unintentional contradiction in policy stemmed from Americans' willingness to sell to both sides in the war and Wilson's unwillingness to stop them from doing so. His insistence on strict neutrality meant there would be no limits placed on US exports to wartime Europe. But such a policy favored the Allies. In the period of US neutrality, the Royal Navy tried to block exports to Germany and protect transatlantic commercial shipping to Britain and France. As a result, US exports to the Allies outpaced those to Germany. Officially neutral, the United States had unwittingly become part of the Allied war effort. *Protection that had US entry*

Germany responded with one of the only means at its disposal: submarine warfare. The German U-boat proved to be a devastatingly effective weapon against both the transatlantic shipping that was sustaining the Allied war effort and the British naval presence that was protecting that shipping. Because US ships were officially neutral, they were also primarily civilian, so the U-boats inflicted a toll on non-combatants. In May 1915, the most dramatic of these incidents occurred when torpedoes fired from a U-boat sank a British passenger liner, the *Lusitania*, resulting in nearly 1,200 civilian deaths, including 128 Americans. Wilson responded with an ultimatum to Germany that it cease the U-boat campaign. The ultimatum worked, but if Germany resumed its submarine warfare, Wilson would have little choice but to abandon neutrality. For this reason, Secretary of State William Jennings Bryan, a fierce opponent of intervention, resigned.

Wilson campaigned for re-election in 1916 on his record of keeping America out of the war, but his policy of neutrality faced its reckoning in the winter of 1917. As that fateful year opened, he called for "peace without victory," but this was untenable to the warring nations who refused to accept that the previous three years had been fought in vain: all sides wanted peace, but they also wanted it with victory for themselves. Then British intelligence intercepted—and quickly leaked to the American press—a secret telegram from the German foreign minister, Arthur Zimmermann, to the government in Mexico City promising help in recovering the territory America took from Mexico in the war of 1846, in exchange for Mexican assistance in keeping the United States preoccupied if it entered the war. Zimmermann was worried about US intervention because Germany had already made the fateful decision to resume unrestricted U-boat warfare in early February. Berlin was right to worry about the American reaction, because it was just about the only thing that would likely tip US public opinion into favoring war with Germany. American entry was now more or less inevitable. The final obstacle fell in March, when the Russian czar, a hated figure in the United States, was overthrown by a liberal, pro-Western revolution. This spared Wilson the awkward dilemma of whether to fight alongside autocratic, czarist Russia.

On April 2, Wilson walked solemnly from the White House to Capitol Hill to request a declaration of war against Germany. Congress complied two days later, and with that the United States officially joined the Great War.

The Wilsonian revolution

Typically, the United States entered the war on its own terms.
Wilson held fast to a key first principle: unilateralism (though
Wilson himself didn't use that word). This was understandable
given how much blood and treasure his nation was about to
commit to solving Europe's problems. If the United States was to
enter the fray, it would do so on its own terms. It was also shrewd,
given how desperate Britain and France were for America's help.
The United States, he explained, would fight alongside the British
and French, but it would not join their alliance. America was not
one of the Allies; instead, it was an Associate. This meant that the
United States fought for its own objectives, which Britain and
France didn't necessarily share. Earlier generations of American
statesmen would have recognized this approach.

Still, they would scarcely have recognized the rest of Wilson's
vision, for the terms on which he brought America into the war
were nothing short of revolutionary. By intervening directly in a
European war, Wilson had made a decisive break with the
tradition of non-entanglement Washington and Jefferson had laid
out over a century before, and with the tradition of separate
hemispheres set out in the Monroe Doctrine. Wilson had made
the world whole, with America entangled at its very center. In
doing so, he set the United States on a totally new course in world
politics: from now on, it would not only play a part, it would have
a starring role.

Wilson explained what he meant in his Fourteen Points, outlined
in a special address to a joint session of Congress in January 1918.
Though many of the points dealt with specific border disputes and
the like, Wilson's Fourteen Points address is rightly regarded as
one of the most important in American diplomatic history,
because it established a totally new set of first principles that, with
a few exceptions, has provided the foundations for America in the
world ever since.

5. John Singer Sargent's portrait of Woodrow Wilson captures his brooding studiousness and boldness of vision. Although it failed in Wilson's day, Wilsonianism was resurrected during World War II and provided the basis for US power in the decades after.

This vision has been known by various names, most commonly "liberal internationalism" and, in honor of its visionary, "Wilsonianism." Even though neither term was in use at that time, they both reflect the worldview that shaped Wilson's war aims. Internationalism differed from the prevailing foreign policy of unilateralism in that it saw the world not merely as interconnected, but as interdependent. What happened in one nation mattered to other nations, with effects that were significant and direct. Internationalists therefore believed that great power brought with it great responsibilities, particularly in helping maintain a smoothly working world order that delivered peace and prosperity. If the United States was to be a great power, it had to behave like one and uphold the tenets of civilization. The basis for a civilized world order would be underpinned by the Wilsonian holy trinity of national self-determination (or what Wilson called "autonomous development"), democracy, and international organization. Beneath that holy trinity were other principles of international openness which Americans of that era prized in particular: equal access to trade, freedom of the seas, and disarmament. In place of secret treaties, Wilson called for "open covenants of peace, openly arrived at." The traditional guarantor of civilized world order had been the great liberal powers of the age, France and (especially) Britain, but by 1917 it was clear to Wilson that the primary duty had fallen to the United States.

Observers at the time found Wilson insufferably moralistic and dismissed his Fourteen Points as woolly-headed idealism. "Moses was satisfied with 10 commandments," French Prime Minister Georges Clemenceau is reported to have joked, "but Wilson requires 14." Historians ever since have joined in the criticism of Wilsonian "idealism." Wilson certainly had a vision, and a revolutionary one at that, but it wasn't unrealistic idealism. He was, the historian John A. Thompson reminds us, a successful politician—governor of New Jersey before becoming a two-term president of the United States—who, like any successful politician, had to be a hard-headed pragmatist. Consider the Fourteen

Points. The most supposedly idealistic of them were in fact direct responses to what Wilson (and most others at the time) saw as the original causes of war in 1914. For example, national self-determination would prevent the outbreak of local rebellions against foreign rule, which had lit the fuse in the Balkans. Freedom of the seas would prevent attacks on neutral shipping, such as the German U-boat campaign in the Atlantic. Open covenants and the League of Nations would forestall the secret alliances and defense pacts, of the kind between Serbia and Russia or Germany and Austria-Hungary, that had committed nations to war even when they had second thoughts. The League would also provide a middle ground for discussing and solving tensions that, if unaddressed and left to fester, would otherwise lead to war.

Wilson's vision wasn't so much one of idealism, then, as an expression of what the historian Arthur Link once called "higher realism." Wilson didn't pursue these objectives as abstract principles of ideal intent. Instead, they were specific tactics designed to address specific concerns. Doing so would hopefully create a better world, but Wilson's overriding objective was to safeguard the interests of the United States in an interdependent world—a world in which Americans could no longer avoid foreign entanglements. In April 1917, when he asked Congress to declare war on Germany, Wilson had urged that the "world must be made safe for democracy." This sounded pious, but was actually grounded in hard-headed statecraft, for making the world safe for democracy would also make it safe for the world's biggest democracy: the United States. If the world order was re-founded on liberal democratic terms, it would mean nothing less than the Americanization of the world.

Whether it was idealistic, realistic, or a subtle combination of the two, Wilson's vision only extended as far as the outer reaches of white, Christian Europe. As Erez Manela has shown, anti-colonial nationalists in Vietnam, India, and elsewhere painfully discovered that Wilson's call for democracy and self-determination did not apply to Europe's sprawling colonial empires. Partly this was because Wilson could hardly force an unwilling Britain and France to decolonize—but it also reflected Wilson's own prejudices. He was not about to give the Philippines or Cuba their independence; he invaded Mexico (twice); and he oversaw the military occupation of the Dominican Republic, Nicaragua, and Haiti. At home, moreover, Wilson supported the imposition of Jim Crow in the South and initiated the racial segregation of federal employees. Wilsonian internationalism was never truly universalistic or consistently applied, but the foreign policies of major powers rarely are.

American intervention in the war proved decisive, but not at first. The US military had a lot of catching up to do. Compared to the large European armies that had been already engulfed in a war for survival for the past three years, the US Army was small, ill-equipped, and untrained. Wilson therefore needed to raise an army, quickly. The buildup over the next year was impressive, helped by the fact that American industry was already in high gear, producing war materiel for Britain and France. A small trickle of soldiers for the American Expeditionary Force (AEF) began to arrive in France in the summer of 1917; a tidal wave of over a million followed, but not until the following spring. Psychologically, however, the entry of the Americans changed the dynamic of the war, for those first waves of AEF soldiers would be followed by wave after wave of soldiers. And their contributions to the campaign of 1918 were important, most notably the key Allied victories at Belleau Wood, Château-Thierry, and Saint-Mihiel. On November 11, 1918, with the battle of the Meuse-Argonne still underway, Germany sued for peace. The Great War was over.

But the Germans were careful not to surrender to the Allies. Instead, as Wilson had hoped, they surrendered to the United States under the terms of the Fourteen Points. This made sense from Berlin's point of view, for Wilson had rejected territorial conquest as a spoil of war. But it made little sense from the perspective of London and Paris, where statesmen had already—in secret—divvied up the German and Ottoman empires (for example, the notorious Sykes-Picot Agreement of 1916, which carved up the Middle East into new British and French protectorates). This difference in perspective among the victorious powers did not augur well for the future.

The peace conference to settle the terms of Germany's defeat met in Paris in the first six months of 1919. Wilson broke with tradition here, too, for he sailed to France to oversee the negotiations himself, thus becoming the first US president to travel to Europe while in office and the first to hold a summit meeting with foreign leaders. He did not, however, bring any Republicans with him, ensuring that whatever deal he made would be divided along highly partisan lines.

Those final terms, fittingly signed in the Hall of Mirrors at the palace in Versailles, were an imperfect compromise between Wilsonianism and the more traditional statecraft of the Allies. Germany was to pay reparations to France and Britain, and it lost some of its territory to the newly independent states of Poland and Czechoslovakia. The war also brought an end to the three empires that had banded together in war: the German, Austro-Hungarian, and Ottoman empires—the latter two mainstays since the early modern period—ceased to exist.

The war had also caused the demise of yet another great empire, the Russian, though its fate was sealed in the streets of St. Petersburg. The Menshevik liberal revolution of March failed to inspire Russians, and it failed to wage war any better than Czar Nicholas II. With unrest growing, the more radical Bolsheviks seized their opportunity and took power in October. Russia, newly christened as the Soviet Union, became the world's first communist power. The Soviets offered a starkly different, indeed rival, internationalism as the basis of world order, one that was illiberal, and based on collective justice and a command economy rather than individual liberty and the free market. This was a momentous development for the United States as well, for the conflict between the rival worldviews of Soviet-led communism and American-led capitalism would define international politics for the next seventy years, beginning with US intervention in the Russian Civil War.

→ caused problems

Wilson was worried by the emergence of communism, but for him the most significant postwar development was the centerpiece of the Treaty of Versailles: the League of Nations. The League was the world's first permanent international organization, the kind of institution for which peace activists had been campaigning for decades. In 1835 the poet Tennyson foresaw a day when "the war-drum throbb'd no longer, and the battle-flags were furl'd/In the Parliament of man, the Federation of the world." That day seemed to have come.

→ poorly balanced

The League enshrined several important principles, among them collective security and the open deliberation of international problems. But it suffered from two fatal, if paradoxical, flaws: it was both too weak and too strong. Its weakness stemmed from the absence of an enforcement mechanism for League decisions. For example, if a state invaded another state—a clear violation of international law—the League had no automatic means of punishing the aggressor. By contrast, the League was also too strong. According to Article X of its founding covenant, the League's decisions were binding upon all members. Its actions therefore overrode the domestic law of its member states— including the US Constitution. Even though Article X's phrasing left some room for flexibility, this was too much for most Republican senators, who had to ratify Wilson's signature to the treaty if it was ever to gain force in the United States. But they

international system of lacked justice

refused to do so as long as Article X of the League of Nations covenant appeared to supersede Article 1, Section 8 of the United States Constitution. By the narrowest of margins, the Senate refused to ratify the Treaty of Versailles, and with that the United States abdicated its leadership role in world politics.

statement bold

Chapter 4
The American century?

Few people have captured the essence of America's rise to globalism as perfectly as Henry Luce. As the founder of some of the nation's most influential magazines, such as *Time* and *Life*, Luce had enormous influence over the way Americans interpreted the world around them. As a successful businessman, he mastered the kind of consumer capitalism that was coming to predominate in the US economy. And as a child of missionaries who had been born in China but educated in the United States, he epitomized America's global perspective.

But by the winter of 1941, Luce found himself increasingly frustrated with his country's situation. Americans had spurned the call to leadership after the Great War, and the rest of the world was paying the price. With France and much of Western Europe under Nazi occupation, Congress debated the Lend-Lease Act, which would effectively donate war supplies to Britain and enable it to maintain its defiance of Germany. At that moment, the fate of Lend-Lease, which internationalists like Luce saw as pivotal to the survival of Western civilization, was still undecided.

With a missionary's dedication to service, and an imperialist's appreciation of power, Luce took it upon himself to reissue that call. Even as the United States grew to become "the most powerful and the most vital nation in the world," he wrote in a February

1941 issue of his flagship magazine, *Life*, "Americans were unable to accommodate themselves spiritually and practically to that fact. Hence they have failed to play their part as a world power—a failure which has had disastrous consequences for themselves and for all mankind. And the cure is this: to accept wholeheartedly our duty and our opportunity as the most powerful and vital nation in the world and in consequence to exert upon the world the full impact of our influence, for such purposes as we see fit and by such means as we see fit." Americans might want to turn their backs on the world, but they simply couldn't. Luce instead called for a new steely-eyed realism; Americans would make the world a better place not simply because it was the right thing to do but because it was the smart thing to do. If the world was to be made safe for America, he concluded, it "must be to a significant degree an American Century."

Luce's call was a breathtaking assertion of American intent, a heady combination of ideals and interests that could serve as a political blueprint for the emergence of the United States as the world's dominant power. Had it been confined to the pages of a popular magazine, it would probably be of limited importance. But it was shared by many other like-minded internationalists— including, crucially, the president of the United States, Franklin D. Roosevelt. Under FDR's watch, the United States transitioned from a major but often peripheral actor on the world scene to one of the most powerful states the world had ever seen.

America in the world

Despite rejecting the internationalist marriage Woodrow Wilson had arranged between the United States and the rest of the world, America was still the strongest state in the international system, and it was still as thoroughly enmeshed in globalization as ever. Americans couldn't avoid the world any more than the rest of the world could avoid America. Even if the United States didn't join the League of Nations (forty-two other countries did), it was still a major political, military, and economic influence on world affairs. Wilsonianism might have been a false start, but American internationalism wasn't yet dead.

We thus need to rethink two pervasive myths about American foreign policy between the world wars. The first is isolationism. While it's true that the United States didn't help plan much of the formal international architecture drawn up after the Great War, it did join other states in the collaborative maintenance of postwar order. In 1921–22, for example, Washington hosted a multinational conference on naval disarmament in the Pacific; three treaties, signed by the United States, Japan, Britain, France, and several other countries, reduced great-power tensions along the Pacific Rim. Americans were active in European politics as well. By revising the payment schedule of reparations from World War I, the 1924 Dawes Plan and the 1929 Young Plan (named, respectively, for the American banker Charles Dawes and the American businessman Owen Young) refinanced Europe's debts and alleviated tensions that could have led to another outbreak of war. And in 1928, Secretary of State Frank Kellogg signed the Pact of Paris, a formal treaty by which states agreed to the "renunciation of war as an instrument of national policy"—in essence, the abolition of war. It's true that some of these initiatives suffered from a lack of enforcement—the wholly idealistic and unworkable Pact of Paris is a particularly egregious example. And it's true that many of them lacked crucial backing from Washington—the refinancing of European debt was done mostly with loans from US banks, not the Treasury, which made them more unstable. But they were hardly the actions of a genuinely "isolationist" power.

The second myth, related to the first, is the supposed trend of deglobalization. Economic historians have done the most to chart the ebb and flow of historical globalization, and their work is enlightening. But it can also be misleading, for if we only measure globalization in terms of economic measurements we miss a great deal. It's certainly true that World War I had an adverse impact on overseas trade, though some sectors of the economy saw a boost of exports to Europe. On top of that, Congress passed a series of bills, culminating in the 1924 National Origins Act, that restricted the legal flow of immigrants into the United States. The flow of goods and people—two of the benchmarks for measuring globalization— didn't recover for another half-century. But as we've seen, the US government was hardly inactive in world affairs in the 1920s. Moreover, private interests and ordinary citizens were ahead of their government in forging links with the rest of the world. This included not only increasingly intimate corporate links with other capitalist nations—General Motors buying German and French automakers, RCA branching out in Britain—but also communist ones.

At a time when Washington still hadn't established official ties with Moscow, the Wall Street investment bank Harriman Brothers (later Brown Brothers Harriman) was lending money to help the Soviet Union embark upon a new program of industrialization, known as the Five-Year Plan. In turn, communist officials found inspiration in Fordism, the manufacturing strategy of Henry Ford's car company. At the same time, American travelers— merchants, missionaries, and tourists—wandered across the world, not just in Europe but throughout Asia, Africa, and Latin America. Americans were also leading the way on transnational cooperation and integration, through initiatives such as the Protestant ecumenical movement that culminated in the founding of the World Council of Churches in 1938 or setting up service organizations, such as the Rotary Club, in other countries. And these were hardly isolated examples—Americans circulated the globe throughout the interwar era. Looking at the sensibility of the era, and not just at trade flows in a fragile world economy, it's clear that Americans were more globally minded than ever.

To be sure, the onset of the Great Depression dealt a blow to globalization, as well as to America's ambitions as a global power. Trade that boomed after the war was decimated by the

Depression. Virtually every development in US foreign policy in the decade after 1929 resulted in either an unwillingness to become involved in new commitments or a withdrawal from existing ones. When Japan invaded and occupied Manchuria in 1931, the United States responded with the Stimson Doctrine, named for Secretary of State Henry L. Stimson, of "non-recognition." This largely symbolic gesture was, much like the Pact of Paris it invoked by way of justification, morally satisfying but totally ineffective. In 1933, newly elected President Franklin D. Roosevelt announced the Good Neighbor Policy of non-intervention in Latin America; pulled the dollar off the gold standard; and withdrew from the London Economic Conference, which sought a multilateral solution to the Depression. In 1935, with tensions mounting in Europe and East Asia, Congress passed the first of a series of Neutrality Acts designed to prevent the United States—and, most notably, its president—from getting sucked into another great-power war. If there was ever an era in which the United States came closest to actually being isolationist, it was the 1930s.

Even so, Americans at the time were hardly isolated, and historians are now reluctant to use "isolationism" as a neutral, descriptive term. For one thing, the term "isolationist" was a political epithet employed to delegitimize critics of foreign entanglements; it didn't come into frequent use until the outbreak of war in Europe in 1939 forced Americans to debate their place in world affairs. For another, many Americans—probably a majority—who didn't want to intervene in Europe's wars were thoughtful internationalists who wanted to extend humanitarian relief and to try to mediate international conflict without getting directly involved in the fighting themselves. They are more properly called "non-interventionists," not isolationists. As Brooke Blower has argued, the era should better be known as one of "neutrality," not isolationism.

These distinctions increasingly mattered in the 1930s, as the rickety world order built in the wake of the Great War began to splinter. The Depression was the greatest source of instability, for it saw the rise to power of fascist and ultra-nationalist regimes in Germany and Japan that wanted to revise the terms of the Versailles Treaty in Europe and the Washington Conference in Asia. The revisionist powers resented Britain, France, and the United States for constructing a new world order at their expense. Fueled by this resentment, they wanted to rearm and go on the offensive.

Japan triggered the onset of a world crisis that would eventually lead to World War II with its seizure of Manchuria in 1931; Italy followed suit with its invasion of Ethiopia, a League of Nations member, in 1935; fascist Spanish troops launched a civil war against the democratically elected government in Madrid in 1936; and the Nazis began a massive rearmament program and remilitarized the Rhineland, both in direct violation of the Versailles terms, that same year.

The crisis escalated in the summer of 1937, when Japan invaded China. In the face of German demands for a large piece of Czech sovereign territory, Britain and France used a summit meeting in Munich to attempt a policy of "appeasement" instead of resorting to war; yet only a few months later, Germany violated the Munich Agreement by dividing Czechoslovakia, sponsoring a new Slovak republic, and conquering the rest of the Czech territory. In late August, Nazi Germany and the Soviet Union signed a non-aggression pact and secretly agreed to divide Poland in two. A week later, on September 1, 1939, Germany invaded Poland, prompting Britain, France, and Canada to declare war on Germany. World War II had begun.

The great debate and the invention of "national security"

The debate over America's proper response to the escalating world crisis unfolded against the steady global retreat of liberalism and capitalism. Whether or not they should be called "isolationists,"

Americans who opposed active involvement in resisting the illiberal onslaught had the upper hand.

That might have been the end of the story, had the internationalists not counted among their number the president of the United States. In his first term, Franklin Roosevelt paid relatively little attention to foreign affairs and embarked on no significant foreign-policy initiatives, aside from officially recognizing the Soviet Union. Everything else, from the Good Neighbor Policy to the maintenance of strict neutrality toward the Spanish Civil War, represented one of the most inactive foreign policies of any modern president.

This inactivity was rooted in what Roosevelt saw as his primary task: pulling America out of the Great Depression. It didn't mean he was untroubled by developments overseas, particularly in Germany and Japan. By 1936–37, Roosevelt's social-welfare program at home, the New Deal, seemed to have had a stabilizing effect, and the US economy showed signs of revival. At the same time, Germany and Japan went on the offensive, prompting FDR to shift his attention from the domestic economic crisis to the international security crisis.

Roosevelt himself believed that the revisionist powers, especially Germany, posed an unprecedented threat to the security and even survival of the United States and its way of life. Beginning in 1937, first with rhetorical resistance and then with more concrete measures, he positioned the United States in an anti-German and anti-Japanese stance. After Japan's invasion of China, Roosevelt called on other countries to "quarantine" the nations aggressively undermining world order. He continued to sound the internationalist alarm over the next few years, as Germany and Japan made further moves into other countries.

Among most Americans, however, Roosevelt's call for a geopolitical quarantine met with little support. Anti-interventionists, mindful of how their country had been sucked into the Great War despite widespread opposition, had public opinion on their side, and they pushed back against the president. Some of FDR's critics, such as Senator Gerald Nye or the famed aviator Charles Lindbergh, fit the isolationist stereotype: Anglophobic, anti-Semitic, and nativist, they resisted virtually any kind of US involvement in the world crisis. Following Lindbergh's leadership, many of them did so under the banner of America First, the largest "isolationist" organization in the country.

Yet most non-interventionists didn't conform to this crude stereotype; they were instead internationalists who renounced war. Their figurehead wasn't a racist like Nye or an anti-Semite like Lindbergh, but rather the former president and ardent humanitarian Herbert Hoover. These non-interventionists argued that the greatest threat to the American way of life was war itself, with all the damage it would inflict upon civil liberties and free markets at home. Their words had an unusual force which the president found difficult to counter, for they had logic on their side: as morally contemptible as it was, Germany lacked the wherewithal to attack the continental United States, much less invade and occupy it. The same was true of Japan. Americans, said Hoover, would be best served by sitting out this conflict, as they should have done in 1917. To Roosevelt's warning that air power rendered America newly vulnerable, Lindbergh had an effective counterargument of his own: air power gave the United States a virtually impregnable defense against a foreign power whose lines of communication, both in the air and at sea, would be thinly stretched across an entire ocean.

The great debate over whether the United States should enter the war marked a watershed in American diplomatic history, for it resulted in the most far-reaching consequences imaginable. To counter the likes of Hoover, Roosevelt and other internationalists stretched the very meaning of self-defense. In a globalized

6. By warning the American people that they couldn't remain isolated when technology was collapsing geographical distance, Franklin D. Roosevelt oversaw a radical change in how Americans saw their place in an increasingly globalizing world. In this photo, from Christmas Day 1942, he inspects a large globe he referred to in his radio addresses.

international system, Americans could no longer assume their geographical position would ensure security, especially when distant adversaries stood for political and economic ways of life that were completely hostile to America's liberal society. Technology and totalitarian ideologies had transformed formerly remote unpleasantries into real and direct threats. Even if those threats weren't imminent, it would be risky to assume they would remain so. America could not live in the modern world all by itself. Without greater action, Roosevelt foresaw the United States becoming "a lone island in a world dominated by the philosophy of force. Such an island may be the dream of those who still talk and vote as isolationists," but to FDR it was "a helpless nightmare of a people without freedom—the nightmare of a people lodged in

71

prison, handcuffed, hungry, and fed through the bars from day to day by the contemptuous, unpitying masters of other continents."

This bit of rhetorical flourish laid the groundwork for possibly the most significant transformation in the entire history of American foreign relations: the national security revolution. Beginning in 1937, Roosevelt spoke less and less about "self-defense" and "the national interest" and more and more about "national security." Strictly speaking, "national security" should simply refer to the security of the nation, and be synonymous with self-defense. Before the world crisis of the late 1930s, this meant the protection of the continental United States' territorial sovereignty from external attack. But Roosevelt felt that this narrower conception of self-defense was antiquated in an era dominated by totalitarian dictators and advanced weaponry. In response, and in order to overcome Americans' reluctance to get involved on a global scale in the absence of a clear and present danger, he vastly broadened the notion of self-defense to include the worldwide protection of America's ideas and values. As FDR put it in his 1939 State of the Union address, "There comes a time in the affairs of men when they must prepare to defend, not their homes alone, but the tenets of faith and humanity on which their churches, their governments and their very civilization are founded." This is what Roosevelt meant by "national security."

It is difficult to overstate the importance of the transition from self-defense to national security. Under the narrower terms of the former, the need for US intervention in world affairs was fairly limited. But, under the sway of the latter, US foreign policy became much more proactive. With the dictates of "national security" ringing in their ears, American leaders would be both constrained and unleashed: constrained in that their discretion over whether to intervene was drastically reduced, and unleashed in that the frequency of their military endeavors was increased. This was because, by expanding the parameters of self-defense, the doctrine of national security raised the stakes of American survival. If America's safety could be threatened from virtually anywhere in the world—by a Japanese encroachment on Indochina, for example, or a German attack on Norway—and if it could be threatened by hostile ideologies as much as by hostile weapons, then achieving an acceptable level of security would be difficult, if not impossible. Under these conditions, any prudent president would have to err on the side of caution and address the threat, no matter how remote or indirect, head-on.

no way to be entirely safe

However, Roosevelt's radical reconceptualization of American security almost didn't take root. His 1939 State of the Union address, much like the "quarantine" and "lone island" speeches and dozens of others just like them, only had a limited effect. And yet, thanks to an unlikely partner, FDR's internationalist vision carried the day. Without the increasingly extremist rhetoric of Adolf Hitler and the spectacular successes his Nazi war machine achieved across Europe, it's unlikely Roosevelt would have been able to persuade his fellow Americans to assume the mantle of world leadership.

As Hitler's armies swept across Europe, FDR's warnings were seen in a new light. In 1939, Germany invaded Poland and annexed half of it (the Soviet Union took the other half). A "phony war" of mostly posturing and strategizing ensued, but German advances resumed in 1940 after the end of winter: Denmark and Norway fell in April, Belgium and the Netherlands in May, and Nazi troops marched into Paris on June 14. Half of France was occupied by German troops, while the other half was ruled by a collaborationist regime based in Vichy. Germany's air force, the Luftwaffe, next turned its sights on Britain, and American correspondents based in London brought the terrifying sounds of the air raid to riveted listeners back home. Yugoslavia and Greece fell in April 1941. In June, the Germans used the element of surprise to invade the Soviet Union, and by the first week of December they were at the gates of Moscow. All of Europe now lay within Hitler's grasp.

A similar onslaught, by Japan, was unfolding at the same time in East Asia. After the initial invasion in 1937, the Japanese had conquered much of China, including virtually all its key ports as well as the major cities of Beijing and Shanghai, by the time German tanks crossed into the Soviet Union in the summer of 1941. After the Japanese seized parts of Indochina, the Roosevelt administration imposed an embargo on exports of oil and other fuels to Japan (this was the first time the United States was drawn into a conflict over Vietnam). The embargo meant that Japan would have to find a replacement source for nearly all its energy needs. It found that source in Europe's resource-rich colonies of Southeast Asia, which the beleaguered European powers were no longer able to defend.

Maybe FDR had been right all along that America couldn't sit this war out. Until the fall of 1941, Americans still debated the issue, though the interventionists now had the momentum. On December 7, 1941, a day which Roosevelt said would "live in infamy," the Japanese raid on the US naval base at Pearl Harbor, Hawaii, put an end to the argument. Hawaii itself wasn't a target for Japanese territorial ambitions, but in order to protect their advances in Southeast Asia they needed to knock out the US Pacific fleet. With 2,403 Americans killed in the attack, the debate over whether to enter the war was over.

Beginning December 8 and continuing through January 1942, Japan invaded and occupied French Indochina, the Dutch East Indies, and British Hong Kong, Singapore, and Malaya. Even Thailand, which had never been colonized, capitulated. In May, Filipino and US forces in the Philippines succumbed after a grueling six-month campaign. Japan now controlled virtually the entire western rim of the Pacific Ocean.

Total war machine

The United States entered World War II as an ally of Great Britain, the Soviet Union, and China. Although the British were to some extent engaged in the Pacific theater, America was the only belligerent fighting on two distinct fronts. It led the invasions of Axis-held North Africa, Italy, and France, and it spearheaded the campaign across the Pacific. Over 16 million Americans did some form of military service. More importantly, American factories produced the goods, from weapons to clothing to foodstuffs, that sustained the Allied war effort. For good reason, Roosevelt described the United States as the "arsenal of democracy." That had been true even before December 1941, when the Lend-Lease program effectively donated millions of dollars of war materiel to Britain and the Soviet Union. Once the United States was at war, aid increased exponentially, and the Allies' eventual victory owed much to America's unprecedented industrial output and to the fact that American industry was far out of range of German and Japanese bombers.

The US military commitment was also critical. In the European theater, Americans fought alongside British and Canadian forces, as well as exiled soldiers from France, the Netherlands, Norway, and Poland. British leaders wanted to avoid repeating World War I's slaughterhouse experience of trench warfare, and they convinced their American counterparts that a frontal assault on Europe was suicidal. Their fears were realized with the disastrous Canadian attempt to land forces at Dieppe, on the French coast, in August 1942. Instead, US and British forces followed a southern detour into Europe, beginning with the invasion of North Africa in November 1942, Sicily in July 1943, and Italy in September 1943. In June 1944, in the famous D-Day landings on the beaches in Normandy, US, British, and Canadian troops successfully broke into Nazi-occupied Europe, and by August they had liberated Paris. The push north into the Low Countries proved more difficult, but in January, after General George Patton relieved besieged US forces in the Ardennes forest during the six-week Battle of the Bulge, a pathway into Germany itself opened up. On the Eastern Front, where fighting was even more brutal and bloody, the Soviet Red Army relentlessly drove the Germans back.

Just as American and British troops were pushing into Germany from the west, the Soviets were pushing from the east. Meanwhile, Allied bombers pummeled Nazi targets across Europe, especially throughout Germany, but also in strategic cities in Nazi-occupied countries. On May 8, 1945, the war in Europe came to an end.

In Asia and the Pacific, the US role was much more predominant—without direct US military involvement, it's doubtful Japan could have been defeated at all. After the Japanese assault on Hawaii and Southeast Asia in December 1941 and January 1942, America and its allies—mainly China, Britain, Australia, New Zealand, and resistance forces scattered across the continent, such as the Viet Minh in Vietnam—were on the defensive. However, in June 1942 the Battle of Midway, in the middle of the Pacific, saw a crushing US naval victory and the significant degrading of Japanese sea power. That enabled US forces to use their superiority in the air and at sea to push the Japanese back across the Pacific. American forces island-hopped their way toward the Philippines, capturing small, isolated spits of land that could act as bases for Japanese planes.

By 1943, the United States had imposed its dominance in the air and was inflicting damage the Japanese couldn't sustain. While American losses were also heavy, the industrial warfare state back home was able to replace them quickly. American forces returned to the Philippines toward the end of 1944 and, with the landings at Iwo Jima and Okinawa in early 1945, began encroaching on the Japanese home islands with the possibility of invading Japan itself by the end of the year. Throughout 1944 and into 1945, US warplanes pounded Japan from the sky. On the continent, Chinese forces started to gain the advantage in their grueling war of attrition against the Japanese occupation. The war came to an end in August 1945, when the Soviet Union joined the Allied campaign and the United States deployed nuclear weapons for the first time in history. The atomic bombing of the Japanese cities of Hiroshima and Nagasaki and an impending US invasion forced

Japan's surrender. The war in Asia and the Pacific ended on
August 15, 1945.

The US war effort was both monumental and consequential, but it
should not eclipse the massive exertions of its allies. The American
contribution to the defeat of Germany, for example, had been
critical without being decisive. It was the Soviets, sustaining
military casualties nearly thirty times greater than US losses in
Europe, who bore the brunt of the Allied campaign; as a
percentage of population, British and Canadian losses were also
marginally greater. And in East Asia, China's armies performed a
similar function to the Red Army in Europe, tying down the bulk
of the enemy's ground forces while the United States entered on
the opposite flank with its advanced military technology in the air
and at sea. American losses were heavy but paled in comparison to
those of the Chinese.

Nonetheless, the American war effort was uniquely impressive in
several respects. Alone among all the belligerents, it had waged a
truly global war on two distinct fronts. Britain had participated in
the war in Asia, but its role there was much smaller than in
Europe. It was American entry into the war, in late 1941, that tied
several regional conflicts together into a single world war, and the
United States was the only country to play a key role in virtually
every one of its far-flung corners. More to the point, without
American entry into the war, it is highly unlikely that the Germans
and Japanese would have been defeated.

The United States was also unique in having escaped the war's
destruction. Just over 400,000 Americans lost their lives in battle,
making it the second-bloodiest war in American history after the
Civil War—but those losses were small compared to the numbers
of troops who perished from Japan (at least 2 million), China (at
least 3 million), Germany (at least 4.5 million), and the Soviet
Union (at least 10 million). An even more telling statistic is the
number of American civilians who died in the war, around 12,000,

compared to the tens of millions of civilians who died in Europe and Asia; figures are inexact, but at least 10 million Chinese and 15 million Soviet non-combatants died. This was because, alone among the belligerents, the United States didn't witness any fighting on its soil. Aside from the raid on Pearl Harbor, the Japanese occupation of two small and remote Aleutian islands, and a handful of isolated and ineffectual Japanese attacks on the west coast of the United States, Americans didn't suffer the aerial bombings, urban warfare, and genocidal bloodshed that were part of the collective experience of people across Europe and Asia; neither did they see their streets, railroads, bridges, hospitals, churches, and factories reduced to rubble. By contrast Britain, which like the United States also avoided invasion and occupation, suffered tremendous damage and civilian casualties as a result of German bombing. In fact, American industry not only avoided any damage, it boomed as a result of the war. The demands of rearmament, not the economic reforms of Roosevelt's New Deal program, brought the United States out of the Depression and into prosperity. The notion that World War II was a time of total domestic harmony and solidarity has rightly been derided as a myth, but in comparison to the experience of virtually every other country, the United States did indeed have "a good war."

The return of Woodrow Wilson

The combination of these two factors—the fact that the outcome of the war was in large part due to US involvement, as well as the fact that the war was a boon to the United States at a time when all its peer competitors had been devastated, physically, financially, and psychologically—was crucial for the development of the postwar world order. By the summer of 1945, Germany and Japan lay in ruins, and even the ostensible victors—Britain, China, France, and the Soviet Union—faced years of major rebuilding efforts. This gave the United States the lead in determining what kind of shape the international system would take. Americans did not, of course, have all the leverage—the outcome of the war had also empowered the Soviet Union, devastated though it was—and Washington couldn't simply dictate terms to the rest of the world. But the war gave Americans the upper hand in Allied planning of the postwar world order. On most issues, others would have to yield to the American viewpoint, whereas Americans rarely yielded to others. The Grand Alliance of the Soviet Union, Great Britain, and the United States had cooperated on an unimaginable scale to defeat a common enemy of unparalleled brutality. But in this partnership, the Americans were first among equals.

Tellingly, only the United States had engaged in sustained postwar planning during the war itself; other countries were too engaged in their struggles for national survival to be able to pay much attention to what would come after the end of the war. In most of the major wartime declarations of postwar objectives, the Allies followed America's lead. This was true of the 1941 Atlantic Charter, the 1942 United Nations Declaration, and the summit conference meetings in Casablanca, Cairo, Malta, Tehran, and Yalta. At a 1944 conference in New Hampshire, America and its allies founded the Bretton Woods system, an international monetary order based on the US dollar. The successor organization to the League of Nations, the United Nations, was established at a conference in San Francisco in the spring of 1945, and delegates agreed its permanent home would be in New York. The idea of the UN was extremely popular among Americans, especially marginalized groups such as African Americans. Yet a more cautious Roosevelt approached the UN as a "realistic Wilsonian," in Warren Kimball's apt phrase: the five victorious powers in World War II—Britain, China, France, the Soviet Union, and the United States—would form the Security Council and each would wield a veto over all UN decisions, and the UN was prohibited from interfering in the domestic sovereignty of its member states. Compared to all this US postwar planning there were no competing British or Soviet initiatives to speak of, aside from a British hope to revive the Commonwealth and a Soviet determination to be in control of Eastern Europe.

Henry Luce had been prescient—1941 did prove to be the beginning of an American century. To be sure, the United States wasn't omnipotent. During the Cold War, the Soviet Union was a close rival, and US military might was later humbled several times. But even if they weren't all-powerful, Americans were the most powerful people in the world. They set the international system's pace and determined its tone and content. Those parts of the world that didn't want to live in an American century still couldn't escape its reach. In fact, it was the character of precisely those clashes in world views that led to the era in which American power came of age: the Cold War.

Chapter 5
Superpower

When World War II ended in 1945, only two great powers remained on the world stage. The United States was clearly the war's only true victor, as it emerged mostly unharmed and prosperous. It had a monopoly on atomic weapons, and held both the most advanced technology (both commercial and military) and near-total worldwide dominance in the air and at sea. Outside of Eastern Europe, there was scarcely a part of the world where the United States couldn't project its power at will.

Only one other state could provide a potential check on American might: the Soviet Union. In Eastern and Central Europe, the Red Army was totally dominant, and throughout the world communist ideology was held in esteem for being the leading anti-fascist, anti-Nazi, and anti-colonial force. From Europe to Southeast Asia, communists were in the vanguard of resistance movements, and in defeating the Nazi war machine on the Eastern Front, the Soviet Union had suffered exponentially greater losses than nearly every other participant in the war. Around the world, Soviet communism had amassed deep reserves of goodwill and admiration.

The gulf in power between these two new geopolitical giants and all other states was so great that the United States and the USSR both earned a new classification: superpower. They simply dwarfed all others. The modern era was the American century, but not entirely so; it was also very much the communist century. Perhaps not coincidentally, both had been born in 1917, in response to the Great War, with liberal internationalism emerging from Wilsonianism and communist internationalism arising out of Leninism. Between them, the Americans and the Soviets held the fate of the world in their hands. If there was to be a just and durable peace after 1945, an understanding between Washington and Moscow would have to be its foundation.

This was not a fanciful idea, unrealistic as it seems in retrospect. After all, the United States, the USSR, and Britain had formed the Grand Alliance, and they cooperated to defeat the Axis powers. They squabbled, certainly, but they also collaborated in waging a complex war on a global scale. Franklin Roosevelt himself went to his grave believing that collaboration could continue into the postwar era, and there's little evidence to suggest that Josef Stalin felt differently.

And yet, collaboration didn't continue. Instead, the world suffered through four decades of existential tension between the Soviets and the Americans. What, then, explains the collapse of the Grand Alliance? Why did Soviets and Americans move from cooperating in a world war to resisting each other in the Cold War?

Taking control

Ideology certainly had much to do with it. As the historian Odd Arne Westad has pointed out, the organizing principles of the American "empire of liberty" and the Soviet "empire of justice" weren't merely different, but entirely oppositional. To Americans, Soviet communism represented the inverse of everything they held dear: people's democracy instead of liberal democracy; collective justice instead of individual rights; a command economy instead of free markets; communalism instead of private property; atheism instead of religion. Despite Stalin's moderation of revolutionary internationalism in the 1930s, communist ideology professed a need to spread. Americans began to see Nazism and communism as more similar than different, and a new term emerged to describe such illiberal systems: totalitarianism. Yet ideology was a necessary condition, not a sufficient cause. After all, Washington had recognized Moscow in 1933, and the two countries had coexisted peacefully ever since. And Americans often had—and still have—alliances with other countries representing different ideologies, be they theocracies or autocracies, as well as tensions with like-minded countries, such as Britain and France.

Circumstances mattered, too, and events had given Americans and Soviets plenty of reason for distrust. American troops had intervened against the Bolsheviks in the Russian Civil War, and Washington had refused to recognize the Soviet Union's legal right to exist for sixteen years. For their part, the Soviets had forfeited their precious little goodwill when Stalin signed a non-aggression pact with Hitler in August 1939 and then invaded Poland from the east while Germany invaded from the west; after conquering half of Poland, the Red Army then invaded blameless Finland. Throughout the period, including during World War II, Soviet agents remorselessly spied on their American (and British) allies. The two sides did form a military alliance, yet didn't actually do any fighting together, whereas British and Canadian troops integrated closely with American forces in Europe and performed numerous joint operations. Of even greater significance was the close Anglo-American integration on matters of intelligence and nuclear weapons: American officials knew of Britain's most closely guarded intelligence secret, the Ultra codebreaking project, and used its information in virtually seamless partnership with their British counterparts; in turn, Britons were invited to work on the Manhattan Project to develop the atomic bomb. There was never any consideration given to inviting the Soviets into such a close confidence. Genuine trust between Washington and Moscow was always rare, and by the end of the war that had mostly disappeared. When there was no longer a common enemy to unite them in fear, Americans and Soviets had no reserves of trust or affection to unite them in the pursuit of peace. Yet countries tolerate the existence of plenty of states they don't trust. Americans and Soviets didn't have to trust each other to agree on sharing the planet peacefully. Distrust was also a necessary condition, but it too wasn't a sufficient cause.

Despite the defensive strategic terms that came to define the conflict—containment, for example, or deterrence—there was nothing passive about the Cold War. It was a contest that both sides entered into on their own initiative. It was an ongoing process with the same objective as any other war: victory. To get the two sides fully engaged in this conflict, something had to catalyze ideology and distrust into an active state of hostility.

The catalyst for both Washington and Moscow was control—or rather, the lack of control. Both countries had wanted to avoid intervention in World War II, and both managed to do so until 1941. Yet both were dragged in against their will after suffering surprise attacks. Both then mobilized their entire societies in order to wage total war. In 1945, then, both were determined never to put themselves in that position again. They would not allow their external environment to change in such a way that made them vulnerable to circumstances beyond their control. They would use their newfound power to be masters of their own fate.

This meant there was almost no room for compromise. As the Allies met periodically in 1945 and 1946 to plan the postwar world, they discovered they each had non-negotiable terms they considered essential for peace, but were actually considered threatening to the other side. This was a classic "security dilemma," in which one side's defensiveness appeared aggressive, leading the other side to take measures it saw as defensive but appeared, in turn, to be aggressive to the other side. Oppositional ideologies and a lack of trust were the perfect catalysts to trigger a Soviet-American security dilemma. Once this cycle of tension began, it was virtually impossible to control, let alone stop.

Origins of the Cold War

The eighteen months following the war were a time of uncertainty for officials in Washington. A new president, Harry Truman, took office upon the death of Roosevelt in April 1945. Truman, a longtime senator from Missouri, had little experience in foreign affairs and, before Roosevelt had chosen him to be vice president only the year before, was little known outside the Capitol.

Even more uncertain were Soviet intentions. At the Yalta summit meeting in February 1945, Stalin had promised Roosevelt that he would agree to hold free and fair elections in Poland after the war. By the end of the year, it was clear that wasn't going to happen, at least not in a way Americans expected. In early 1946, Stalin gave a major speech in which he seemed to suggest a third world war was coming, this time against the capitalist powers of the West. Through to the end of 1946, Moscow increased its control of governments in countries occupied by the Red Army, demanded that Turkey allow Soviet control of strategic waterways connecting the Black Sea to the Mediterranean, and refused to withdraw its troops from northern Iran, as promised during the war.

After this period of uncertainty, Truman and his advisers acted decisively. There is no official starting date for the Cold War, but a good point of origin is March 12, 1947, and the Truman Doctrine. In a speech to a special joint session of Congress, Truman warned that Greece and Turkey were at risk of falling to the communists. Normally the Near East would be in Britain's sphere of influence, but the British were mired in an economic crisis. Indeed, all of Western Europe was still shattered from the war. A power vacuum, caused by British and French weakness against a backdrop of widespread continental poverty, homelessness, and starvation amid damaged buildings, broken factories, and ruined farms might give the communists the opportunity they needed to seize power. Americans had tried to avoid the last two European wars but could not. Truman felt he couldn't make that same mistake again. Instead, he opted for a strategy the historian Melvyn Leffler has aptly called "a preponderance of power." If America was to be the master of its own fate, it would have to take the initiative and trigger a conflict with the Soviets that fell just short of armed conflict: in other words, the Cold War.

The Truman Doctrine was the first move in this strategy. Truman needed to convince Congress to appropriate funds and, by extension, convince the American people to support an indefinite anti-communist crusade. He did it by doing what all presidential foreign-policy doctrines have done: justify a specific policy for a particular crisis in the name of a general and abstract principle. Just as a crisis involving Greece and Turkey had moved James Monroe to issue his separate-hemispheres doctrine in 1823, Truman used the situation in the Near East to issue a universalist call to arms that had global relevance. Truman did not once mention Stalin or the Soviet Union by name, but it was clear whom he had in mind. "At the present moment in world history nearly every nation must choose between alternative ways of life," he declared. "One way of life is based upon the will of the majority, and is distinguished by free institutions, representative government, free elections, guarantees of individual liberty, freedom of speech and religion, and freedom from political oppression. The second way of life is based upon the will of a minority forcibly imposed upon the majority. It relies upon terror and oppression, a controlled press and radio, fixed elections, and the suppression of personal freedoms." Then came the essence of the Truman Doctrine that would provide the lodestar for US foreign policy for the next forty-five years: "I believe that it must be the policy of the United States to support free peoples who are resisting attempted subjugation by armed minorities or by outside pressures."

Rhetorically, "to support free peoples who are resisting attempted subjugation" was a cumbersome way of introducing the core concept of America's Cold War: containment. This was the brainchild of a previously anonymous diplomat, George F. Kennan, who was posted to the embassy in Moscow. The Truman administration may have been floundering indecisively back in Washington, but from Kennan's perspective in Moscow it seemed clear what was going on in the Soviet Union. Stalin believed in a mix of traditional czarist nationalism and ambitious revolutionary communism. Above all, he dealt in the currency of power. Establishing liberal norms for a more open world meant nothing to Stalin; what he wanted was territory and unchallenged power over it. Stalin was, like the czars before him, an expansionist. But because he understood power, and wanted above all to protect his own power, he could be deterred—if American leaders showed their determination to deter him. This was the essence of Kennan's strategy of containment, expressed first in a top-secret "Long Telegram" to the State Department in February 1946 and, after Truman had decided to make it the basis of US policy, published under the pseudonym "X" in the July 1947 issue of the journal *Foreign Affairs*. As Kennan put it in the public article, instead of either acceding to Stalin's every demand or risking all-out war, the United States should instead adopt a "long-term, patient but firm and vigilant containment of Russian expansive tendencies...designed to confront the Russians with unalterable counter-force at every point where they show signs of encroaching upon the interests of a peaceful and stable world."

In between the Truman Doctrine and the X article came two other important measures designed to give containment substance and strength. The first, a massive aid package to Europe, was announced by Secretary of State George C. Marshall in June 1947. By the time it ended in 1952, the Marshall Plan, officially known as the European Recovery Program, had given away billions to kick-start industrial recovery and ward off starvation, unemployment, anarchy—and communism. Crucially, the money had few strings attached, and recipients were able to put the money toward almost any purpose they wanted, including setting up comprehensive social-welfare states that US taxpayers would never have countenanced back home. This generosity had the ulterior motive of making Western Europe economically dynamic, strongly anti-communist, and loyally allied to the United States. It also helped allay fears in Washington and New York that the end of the war would see a return of the Depression.

The second building block for containment came the next month, when Congress passed the National Security Act. This single piece of legislation established (or provided the basis for) the Central Intelligence Agency, the Joint Chiefs of Staff, the National Security Council (NSC), and the Department of Defense. In other words, the Act created the national security state, and over the years this increasingly complex and secretive institutional apparatus for waging the Cold War would come to shape the contours of American life itself. In 1952, the establishment of the National Security Agency put the final piece of the national security state in place.

Despite Kennan's later claims otherwise, "counter-force" implied that containment would have a significantly militarized character. By creating permanently mobilized services for the use of armed force, intelligence, and espionage, the National Security Act ensured it. So too did the passage of the Selective Service Act in 1948, which instituted the first-ever permanent peacetime military draft in US history. The next year, the founding of the North Atlantic Treaty Organization (NATO) marked the first-ever permanent alliance in US history. This represented a fundamental break in the American diplomatic tradition: unilateralism wasn't yet dead, but it had to share space with an increasingly robust internationalism. Another significant milestone came in April 1950, when the NSC staff filed its sixty-eighth report. Known simply as NSC-68, this document divided the world into half-slave and half-free and predicted that the two couldn't coexist. This wasn't mere rhetoric designed to sway public opinion—NSC-68 was top secret and not declassified until 1975—but rather, an expression of the genuine fear inside the Truman administration. NSC-68's most important consequence was its recommendation to triple defense spending, which raised US military expenditures to around two-thirds of the federal government's overall budget.

Korean War, global Cold War

The authors of NSC-68 had originally presented their report in April 1950, but Truman thought it called for too much, too soon. He feared the onset of such massive military spending on an indefinite basis and shelved the report. What made him change his mind in the five months between April and September?

The answer was found not in Washington or even in Moscow, but on the Korean peninsula, until then a region peripheral to American interests. Korea had been a Japanese colony from 1905 to 1945. To maintain order after World War II, Soviet troops moved into northern Korea, while US troops occupied the peninsula's southern half. Their presence roughly overlapped with the balance of Korean nationalist forces who had been fighting Japanese colonial rule: communist forces held the north, while anti-communist forces dominated the south. But all were Korean nationalists, and with the Japanese gone the struggle turned to who would rule an independent Korea. The informal division of the country began to assume a permanent character with the founding of separate governments in 1948. By previous agreement, Soviet and US occupying forces withdrew from Korea, leaving local leaders to sort out their differences. Communists in the north, led by Kim Il-sung, invaded the south in June 1950, and US troops immediately came to the aid of what was now being called South Korea.

The outbreak of war in Korea, and especially Truman's decision to defend South Korea, had two momentous consequences. First, it globalized the Cold War. Mao Zedong's Chinese Communist Party had taken power in Beijing in October 1949, but Truman and his advisers didn't panic; in fact, they presciently foresaw that the People's Republic of China would eventually become a rival to the Soviet Union. Just as the Japanese attack on Pearl Harbor fused distinct regional conflicts into a single world war, the North Korean invasion set in motion a chain of events that integrated previously far-flung disputes into an interconnected global conflict. Second, the Korean War militarized US foreign policy. The war convinced Truman and his officials that a worldwide communist conspiracy was on the march and that the only way to stop it was to make containment as firm as possible. For the same reasons, the war terrified the American people and aggravated an anti-communist witch hunt at home, a movement better known as McCarthyism—which in turn further intensified the US commitment to a hard version of containment. In addition to tripling the defense budget, as outlined in NSC-68, in 1952 the US detonated the world's first thermonuclear weapon, hundreds of times more powerful than the atomic bombs dropped on Japan.

The end of the Korean War in 1953 came only a few months after Truman left office and Stalin died of a stroke. By then, the world was splitting roughly into three camps: the Soviet-led communist world; the American-led liberal capitalist world, or the so-called "free world"; and the Third World, so-called because its members, such as India and Indonesia, refused to join either of the first two worlds. The interstitial zones where these worlds met—on the Korean peninsula, in Southeast Asia, in the Middle East, and throughout Africa and Latin America—led to collisions that produced what the historian Paul Chamberlin calls "the Cold War's killing fields." The Cold War also gave rise to a new phenomenon of modern sovereignty: divided statehood. Korea and Vietnam were divided into northern and southern halves, each claiming to be the one true embodiment of the nation as a whole; Germany was divided into east and west along the same lines; and so was China, which saw the island shard of Taiwan,

7. In 1945, the United States became the world's first nuclear power. While this new technology brought with it many advantages, it also instilled fear and anxiety—even, as we see from these kneeling soldiers from the 11th Airborne Division witnessing a 1951 atomic test in the Nevada desert, in those who would fight with it.

fragmented from the main body when anti-communist Nationalist forces who lost the Chinese Civil War fled there in 1949, challenge the People's Republic.

The end of empire

The war in Korea was a direct product of superpower tensions, but the conflict between different visions of Korean nationalism was also the result of another phenomenon that intertwined with, yet was independent from, the Cold War: decolonization. The era of European domination of the rest of the world, which had begun in 1492 and continued into the twentieth century, was drawing to a close.

World War II weakened colonial empires throughout Asia and Africa. The Japanese turfed out Britain from Malaya (now Malaysia), Singapore, Hong Kong, and Burma (Myanmar); the Netherlands from the Dutch East Indies (Indonesia); France from Vietnam, Cambodia, and Laos; and the United States from the Philippines. Even where European empires held off the Japanese advance, as in British-ruled India, the aura of imperial authority was shattered—along with the financial and military resources needed to keep the empire secure. Then the Allies won the war, bringing Japan's own colonial regimes in Manchuria, Korea, and Taiwan to an end. When the Japanese were eventually defeated, they left behind a power vacuum in all of these countries that anti-colonial, pro-independence nationalist movements were eager to fill. In prewar East Asia, only China, Japan, and Thailand had not been colonized; after the war, Europe's empires struggled to resurrect their authority, and within little more than a decade the continent was mostly self-governing.

Europeans turned away from their colonial empires, often reluctantly—Portugal, the last major imperial state to divest its major holdings, didn't do so until the 1970s, and then only under gunfire—and instead turned inward to build a new Europe. In

Western Europe, US allies formed the core of what would become a European community and, eventually, the European Union. This massive free-trade zone morphed in the 1990s into a serious project of political and monetary integration. As a spur to economic growth—recovery in the thirty years after the war was dubbed a "miracle"—and political cooperation, the European project enjoyed strong support from the United States because it kept Europeans from killing each other at the same time as it created booming democratic states that were also robustly anti-communist. From Washington's standpoint, there could not have been a better substitute for retrograde empires than continental integration.

The messy process of decolonization produced another major flashpoint, this time in the Middle East. In 1948, the British quit their mandate of Palestine, which had once been a province of the Ottoman Empire but had been in British hands since the end of World War I. Zionists in Palestine announced the birth of the Jewish state of Israel, and Truman extended US recognition only eleven minutes later. He did so against the advice of both the State Department and the Pentagon, which argued that American interests called for prudence in the face of unanimous Arab opposition, at a time when Arab states were becoming a key source of the world's oil. Truman went ahead anyway, even as he, and later Eisenhower, brought the United States into closer partnership with Arab oil producers. It says much about the hegemonic role the United States had assumed by mid-century that it forged two of its closest partnerships, with Israel and Saudi Arabia, at around the same time, even though these two nations had an intense regional and sectarian rivalry.

The Cold War induced decolonization elsewhere, too—even in the United States. After slavery ended with the Civil War, whites in the American South created a new racial hierarchy commonly known as Jim Crow. This rigidly segregated society kept whites and blacks apart, with white superiority legally enshrined. African

Americans were denied a range of constitutional rights, among them the right to vote, and were kept in a state of economic subservience. Black activists had been campaigning for an end to Jim Crow since the turn of the century, but with little success. But the Cold War gave their cause an unexpected boost. The United States now portrayed itself as the leader of the "free world" and referred to Soviet communism as "slavery," yet those claims rang hollow when US citizens were denied basic rights simply because of the color of their skin. The Soviets prominently featured American segregation in their propaganda, but dozens of other countries around the world, many of them newly independent African nations and not all of them allies of the Soviet Union, also took notice. In the Cold War, waged in large part over image, Jim Crow segregation was a serious weakness. Traditionally reluctant to push racial reform on the South, Washington was finally prompted into supporting civil rights reform in order to stave off these communist political attacks. The turning point came in 1957, in Little Rock, Arkansas, when black students tried to attend class in a previously all-white high school. With the ugly scenes of conflict relayed around the world, President Dwight Eisenhower sent in the National Guard to ensure school desegregation in Little Rock. From that point on, foreign pressure and Cold War imperatives gave the civil rights movement much-needed leverage in its struggle for freedom at home.

The crisis years

A decade after it began, the Cold War reached an equilibrium of tension and terror. The bipolar world, finely balanced between American and Soviet power yet often disturbed by unforeseen events in decolonizing or nonaligned regions, had become a system with its own propulsive logic. Rebellions broke out against communist rule in East Germany (1953) and Hungary (1956), and a brief war over the Suez Canal broke out in 1956, with Israel, Britain, and France arrayed against Egypt, but little could divert the course of the Cold War itself.

That all changed in the crisis years from 1958 to 1962, when unresolved tensions in Europe combined with the revolutionary fervor of decolonization to produce a dangerous period of instability. Even though the United States and the Soviet Union remained the most powerful states after the crisis years had subsided, the world they inhabited was no longer as responsive to their demands.

The onset of the crisis years unfolded in a familiar venue: the divided city of Berlin. Once the capital of Germany, Berlin was split into eastern and western halves, just like Germany itself. Soviet premier Nikita Khrushchev and Eisenhower held a summit in Paris in 1960 to resolve the standoff, but Khrushchev stormed out when Soviet air defenses shot down an American U-2 spy plane flying over Russia.

This is where things stood when John F. Kennedy replaced Eisenhower in January 1961. Kennedy seriously considered military action in Berlin, even at the risk of triggering a nuclear exchange, and US and Soviet tanks faced off across Checkpoint Charlie with their guns fixed on one another. But the real pressure was on Khrushchev. Berlin's entire importance stemmed from its symbolism, particularly as a microcosm of the successes of liberal capitalism and the failures of communism, for which an ongoing flood of refugees into West Berlin provided powerful evidence. In August, Khrushchev decided to authorize the construction of a barrier between the two halves of the city. The makeshift wooden fences and barbed wire that went up during the night of August 13, 1961, stopped the flow of people and brought the war scare to an end. Bricks and mortar came shortly after, and the Berlin Wall, as it came to be known, quickly symbolized the Cold War itself. JFK was quietly relieved at Khrushchev's brutal but swiftly definitive action. "A wall is a hell of a lot better than a war," he remarked to an aide.

Berlin wasn't even the most serious war scare Kennedy faced— that came a year later, in Cuba. The island had been an American colony in all but name between the war with Spain and the Good Neighbor Policy, and even afterwards still remained economically beholden to the United States. In 1953, Marxist-influenced revolutionaries led by Fidel Castro mounted a challenge to the country's dictator, Fulgencio Batista. Six years later, the revolutionaries took power in Havana and began to appropriate foreign-owned businesses, mostly those in American hands. As Castro consolidated power and moved further to the left, Kennedy authorized an invasion of the island by anti-Castro Cuban exiles that was secretly sponsored and organized by the United States. The 1,400-strong invasion force, which landed at the ominously named Bay of Pigs in April 1961, was no match for Castro's greater force of battle-hardened troops, and Kennedy resisted intense pressure to rescue the invasion with overt US intervention.

The Bay of Pigs was an embarrassment for the Kennedy administration, which looked not just imperialistic and hypocritical but, perhaps most damagingly of all, weak and incompetent. The fiasco heaped further pressure on JFK, but it also had the more serious consequence of pushing Castro firmly into the Soviet bloc. Castro was a left-wing nationalist revolutionary, but even as late as 1961 had not come out as a committed communist. That ambiguity disappeared after the Bay of Pigs, especially once Kennedy launched a sustained program of economic warfare against Cuba codenamed Operation Mongoose.

To ward off another invasion, and also to redress the strategic inferiority of the Soviet Union, Khrushchev agreed to Castro's request to base Soviet nuclear missiles in Cuba. The Soviet navy began covertly shipping the weapons to Cuba in the late summer of 1962. A U-2 spy plane flying over Cuba captured photos of the missiles being installed on the island, and JFK was alerted of the news on the morning of October 16.

For good reason, the Cuban Missile Crisis has gone down in history as the moment when the world came closest to annihilation. There were numerous moments when the three sides—American, Soviet, and Cuban—almost traded blows, which would in turn almost certainly have led to a wider war. Kennedy felt he couldn't accept the presence of Soviet missiles in Cuba, even though he agreed with his NSC that they posed no additional strategic threat. Yet JFK didn't want to look weak in front of America's Cold War enemies—and he most certainly didn't want to lose face at home, especially with congressional midterms only a few weeks away. So for largely symbolic political reasons, he decided to make a stand and run the risk of war. As Soviet ships approached the island, the US Navy imposed a naval blockade (and euphemistically called it a "quarantine," because a blockade is legally an act of war) and demanded that all vessels stop and be searched. After a few days of high tension and frantic secret negotiations, the Soviet ships turned around. In return, the United States publicly vowed not to invade Cuba and privately agreed to withdraw its own nuclear-tipped Jupiter missiles from Turkey. Their roles had reversed from the Bay of Pigs episode a year before: now it was Kennedy's turn to look statesmanlike and Khrushchev's to look clueless.

Ironically, the resolution of the Cuban Missile Crisis led both sides into a fifteen-year period of relative peace and calm, at least in their relations with each other, known as détente. Though Richard Nixon would oversee its most ambitious phase, it was Kennedy who inaugurated this new working relationship. Washington and Moscow had teetered at the brink of worldwide destruction, and swore never to do it again. In 1963, with the terrifying memory of Cuba still fresh in their minds, they set up a secure telephone hotline to settle crises more quickly and directly; they also signed the Partial Test Ban Treaty, which despite its limited connotations was actually a fairly comprehensive prohibition on testing nuclear weapons in the atmosphere. "For, in the final analysis," JFK proclaimed in a June 1963 speech now seen as the onset of détente, "our most basic common link is that we all inhabit this small planet. We all breathe the same air. We all cherish our children's future. And we are all mortal."

That year, Secretary of Defense Robert S. McNamara pronounced the existence of a doctrine called Mutual Assured Destruction (with the fitting acronym of MAD), which meant that each side could deter the other from aggression, because both sides knew a war would be suicidal. As mad as it seems, the advent of nuclear weapons actually brought an end to the era of total war and made the Cold War an era of superpower peace. The cruelest irony, however, lay in the fact that just as détente was settling in, the United States embarked upon a long and disastrous war in Southeast Asia.

Vietnam

Détente lasted until superpower tensions reemerged from hibernation in the late 1970s. But until then, relations between Moscow and Washington were governed by a shared vision to manage their differences constructively, through diplomacy and direct contacts. And yet this led to the war in Vietnam, which lasted from the early 1960s until the communist victory in 1975. Why did the Cold War's bloodiest conflict occur at precisely the moment its main antagonists had declared a truce?

The main reason was the fact that détente did not end the Cold War; it was merely a process to manage tensions, not put them to rest. Because of this, the fact that the superpowers came so close to nuclear war over Berlin and Cuba actually increased the likelihood of a war over Vietnam. It was clear that tensions in Europe and the Caribbean had to be tamed in order to prevent a third world war from breaking out and destroying the planet. But nuclear weapons weren't part of military strategy on either side in Vietnam, so the chances of the conflict spreading globally were much smaller. And while détente saw a reduction in tensions, it also meant that both sides had to shore up their credibility where they could. Kennedy and his successor, Lyndon B. Johnson, feared that the Soviets would see weakness in a general American retreat from its commitments, which would in turn reduce the effectiveness of détente and lead the Soviets to take increasingly reckless gambles that would bring the world back to where it was in Berlin in 1961 and Cuba in 1962. Perversely, then, in the minds of US officials détente actually rested on maintaining a hard line in places like Vietnam.

Another reason the Vietnam War coincided with détente was that, while Washington had resolved to lower tensions with Moscow, Beijing was another matter. Drawing the line against communist expansion in Vietnam had always been about containing the Chinese, much more so than the Soviets. Events in Vietnam in 1962–63 marked the outbreak of the American phase of the war (also known as the Second Indochina War), which both signaled the beginning of détente and the terminal decline of the alliance between the world's two main communist powers. The Sino-Soviet split, which had begun to show in the 1950s, cracked wide open in 1962. It too was a product of the Cuban Missile Crisis, which Chinese premier Mao Zedong saw as an abject humiliation of the socialist cause worldwide. He vowed not to be so weak. As China became more determined to resist the moderation of the Cold War, the United States became more determined to resist China. One of the places the two actually faced each other was Vietnam.

America's war in Vietnam can also be explained by the weight of prior commitments. The struggle for Vietnam had gone through phases, the First Indochina War being the conflict between France and the communist-led Viet Minh from 1946 to 1954. Washington entered the conflict in 1950, in support of anti-communists in southern Vietnam. In 1954, at the Geneva Conference to settle the terms of France's defeat, the United States forced through the partition of Vietnam at the 17th parallel, with a noncommunist South governed from Saigon and a communist North governed from Hanoi. Against the spirit of the accords signed in Geneva, which called for the reunification of the country under national elections within two years, the United States launched a process of "nation-building" to make South Vietnam an independent country. It was around this time that Eisenhower explained US policy by way of the "domino theory"—the idea being that, if Vietnam fell to communism, it would set off a chain reaction not unlike the toppling of a row of dominoes, and then much of Asia would become communist.

Thus, by the time Kennedy became president in 1961, the United States had in some form committed to upholding a divided, noncommunist South Vietnam for a decade. This doesn't mean that the outbreak of an American war was inevitable—there were plenty of people in Washington, throughout the Kennedy and Johnson administrations as well as in both houses of Congress, not to mention the media, who advised against intervention as early as 1961. But it does mean that these antiwar advocates were arguing against the momentum of recent history.

The same year Kennedy became president, the recently formed National Liberation Front for Vietnam (NLF, commonly known as the Vietcong, or VC) launched a highly effective insurgency against the Saigon government. JFK responded by increasing US military support for South Vietnam, and, by the time he was assassinated in November 1963, there were over 16,000 US military "advisers" in the country. That same month, in a coup covertly supported by the United States, a group of South Vietnamese army generals murdered the country's president, Ngo Dinh Diem. Diem had antagonized the country's Buddhist majority, prompting horrific scenes of protest such as Buddhist monks burning themselves alive. Even worse from Washington's perspective, Diem had begun to send secret peace feelers to Hanoi and the NLF.

The overthrow of Diem instigated severe political instability in Saigon, which the insurgency was only too happy to take advantage of. Simultaneously, the assassination of Kennedy thrust Lyndon Johnson into the White House, and although he had his doubts about whether the United States could prevail, at least at an acceptable cost, he also feared the consequences of turning his back on a commitment upheld by Truman, Eisenhower, and Kennedy before him.

The insurgency continued to make gains through 1964, and by February 1965 it was becoming clear that unless the United States did something drastic, there was a strong possibility South Vietnam would fall. Faced with the agonizing choice of either escalation or withdrawal—both had enormous costs and few obvious benefits—Johnson opted for what he saw as the least-bad option of escalation. A large-scale bombing campaign against North Vietnam, appropriately codenamed Operation Rolling Thunder, began on March 2, and the first US ground troops, a battalion of marines, waded ashore at Danang less than a week later. If the South Vietnamese couldn't win the war, Johnson would Americanize it—that is, take it over from the South Vietnamese.

Johnson's two most important advisers, General William Westmoreland (who commanded the war from Saigon) and Secretary of Defense McNamara, relied on America's overwhelming superiority in military technology and firepower. Westmoreland had an appreciation for the complexities of counterinsurgency, but it did him little good in a conflict where the United States faced so many major disadvantages. One facet of this strategy was the massive aerial bombardment of both Vietnams, North and South, of which Rolling Thunder was only the most prominent campaign. By the end of the war, the United States had dropped more bomb tonnage on Vietnam than all belligerents had dropped worldwide during World War II—and that's not even including the millions of tons of bombs dropped on Laos and Cambodia. In fact, during the war the United States bombed the territory of its ally in the South more than its enemy in the North, which speaks volumes about the perverse logic of US strategy. Another facet was Westmoreland's strategy on the ground in the South, commonly known as "search-and-destroy." The third and final pillar of US strategy was what Johnson dubbed "the other war," an effort to pacify the South Vietnamese countryside and neutralize communist propaganda by effecting positive social change, such as land reform.

Following the Tet Offensive in early 1968, Johnson realized that the war had stalemated and feared that he couldn't win reelection in November. He announced his decision not to run again, halted Rolling Thunder, and entered into negotiations with Hanoi in Paris. With the US commitment to South Vietnam now fatally undermined, Richard Nixon won the presidential election in November on vague assurances to end the war.

The tactical complexities of the fighting, the many civilian casualties and American fatalities that resulted, and the humiliating stalemate all cast a shadow over the war. More damaging was the war's perceived immorality. Johnson stressed that he had to contain the spread of communism and defend democracy and self-determination, but the Vietnamese people themselves seemed more supportive of the communist North than their own corrupt government in Saigon. As a result, millions of Americans protested what their government and the military were doing in Indochina. The anti-Vietnam War movement, the largest war protest in human history, mobilized millions of people in a series of mass demonstrations across the country. Thousands marched through the streets of Washington, and several of the nation's leading universities—including Berkeley, Wisconsin, Michigan, Columbia, and Cornell—came to a standstill due to antiwar activism.

Yet still the war continued—largely, and counterintuitively, as the result of Nixon's strategy to end it. The Vietnam War was full of ironies, but perhaps none was as sharp as Nixon's plan to

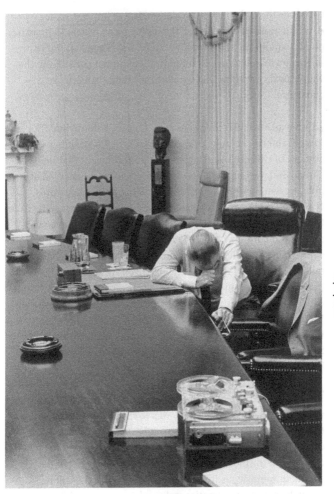

8. President Lyndon B. Johnson waged war in Vietnam reluctantly. By 1968, when this photo was taken, the war had ruined his presidency and torn the nation apart. Here, LBJ is listening to a recording of his son-in-law, the future US Senator Charles Robb, but at the time a US Marine in South Vietnam.

withdraw through massive escalation. It was imperative, for domestic reasons and because the military had reached a breaking point, to pull US forces out of Vietnam. But it was also imperative, in Nixon's mind at least, that South Vietnam not perish from the withdrawal symptoms that would surely follow America's departure.

Nixon explained his strategy as one of "peace with honor." By "peace," though, he didn't mean the absence of war, simply the absence of US boots on the ground. "Honor" meant that the United States would keep its promise to ensure the survival of an independent, noncommunist South Vietnam. In other words, Nixon sought the exact same objective his predecessors going back to Harry Truman had pursued. The trick would come in actually pulling it off, for how would Nixon achieve the same goal that had eluded Johnson, when Johnson had at his disposal over half a million US troops? Nixon's principal means of squaring this circle was called "Vietnamization," marking a reverse course of Johnson's Americanization of the war in 1965. As US troops withdrew, South Vietnamese troops would take their place. This required yet more US economic and military assistance to Saigon, resulting in tiny South Vietnam having one of the largest militaries in the world by 1975.

Nixon deployed two other audacious maneuvers to win the war without American soldiers. One was to expand the bombing campaign against North Vietnam and extend it to previously off-limits targets in Laos and Cambodia. The other was to embark upon one of the most imaginative diplomatic strategies of the twentieth century: institutionalizing détente with the USSR, through arms-control treaties and regular summits, while simultaneously opening up to China after two decades of mutually hostile nonrecognition. The rationale was that, with the Sino-Soviet split wide open, Moscow and Beijing feared each other more than they feared Washington, which in turn gave Nixon, and his chief strategist Henry Kissinger, the leverage they needed. Both

9. In 1972, the United States and the People's Republic of China embarked upon a new partnership that changed world politics forever. President Richard Nixon traveled to Beijing, where he shook hands with Mao Zedong, a leader who had been, until then, America's most bitter enemy.

communist powers, Nixon and Kissinger assumed, would then curry favor with Washington by pressuring Hanoi to end, or at least pause, its campaign in the South.

The main problem, however, was that none of these stratagies actually worked. Vietnamization created a large but ineffective South Vietnamese military, which was easily overrun by the battle-hardened and motivated North Vietnamese. Expanded bombing simply destabilized all of Indochina, without doing sufficient damage to the communist war effort. And while diplomacy worked in creating new, productive relationships, it did nothing to ease Soviet or Chinese support for the North Vietnamese—who, with victory finally in sight, resisted such pressure anyway.

In January 1973, Kissinger signed a peace deal with his North Vietnamese counterpart, Le Duc Tho, in Paris, and by April the last US troops had left South Vietnam. Almost exactly two years later, on April 30, 1975, North Vietnamese tanks rolled into Saigon. Peace had finally come to Vietnam, but it brought no honor to the United States.

Globalization 2.0

The end of the Vietnam War was a significant moment, especially in removing a cancerous issue that had crippled US foreign policy and ruined America's international reputation, but in the long term the more consequential development was Nixon's opening to China. Although it would take another six years for Washington and Beijing to normalize official relations, Sino-American rapprochement immediately reordered the international system along lines that would, for better or worse, determine the course of world politics for at least the next four decades.

Beneath the surface, even larger structural changes were occurring. The most important was the acceleration of the next round of globalization, a process that began maturing in the early twentieth century only for the successive crises of the world wars, the Great Depression, and the early Cold War to stunt its growth. Globalization came roaring back in the late 1960s and into the 1970s as countries in the West continued to liberalize trade among themselves, and then extended those free-trade arrangements with the emerging economies of the Global South, particularly in East and Southeast Asia. As manufacturing began to migrate to those regions, as well as to Latin America, the US economy deindustrialized and became more tertiary and consumerist in orientation. In response, Washington began the gradual deregulation of the US economy, most notably financial services, which further allowed for the freer flow of goods and capital. So too did the advent of new technologies—the personal computer, more powerful computing systems for businesses, robotics that replaced human labor—and modes of transportation, such as the spread of intercontinental jet travel and standardized container shipping. The new geopolitics played a part in facilitating the return of globalization as well, with the end of the war in Vietnam, the opening to China, and the deepening and broadening of European integration all fueling the growth of global interconnections.

Globalization also gave rise to an internationalist doctrine, that of human rights, that changed the way America conducted its foreign relations. Human rights was not an entirely new concept: American missionaries and other religious figures had been calling for a foreign policy based on the dignity of the individual for over a century; presidents such as Wilson and Franklin Roosevelt had launched crusades against tyranny and oppression; the UN had enshrined the notion at the heart of world politics in its 1948 Universal Declaration of Human Rights; and the ideology of containment was grounded in a reaction to communist violations of individual freedoms. But before the 1970s, human rights was more of a slogan than a mission, and it was by no means the basis of a popular crusade that in turn affected US foreign policy. That began to change in the 1970s. In 1975, the United States, Soviet Union, and thirty-three other countries signed the Helsinki Accords, which included the protection of individual human rights as a core principle. In January 1977, newly elected President Jimmy Carter prominently featured human rights in his inaugural address, and he followed through by placing the issue at the center of his foreign policy.

Into the desert

The end of the war in Vietnam, as well as the opening to China, also saw America's strategic gaze shift westward. This was the third zone of crisis to preoccupy the United States since 1914, with the focus falling initially on Europe, then shifting to East and Southeast Asia, and then shifting again to the Middle East. Europe and Asia remained vital interests, but by the 1970s had ceased to be zones of urgent crisis.

While the Middle East had always been important to US interests, at least since World War II and the rise of Saudi oil power, it hadn't before been a central concern. That began to change in June 1967, with the Six Day War between Israel and the Arab states surrounding it (Egypt, Syria, and Jordan). Israel's stunning, quick victory transformed its strategic relationship with the United States, which until then had been polite without being warm or close. Once Israel showed its capability to survive against enormous odds, it became a key asset in the Cold War. Crucially, American popular support for Israel soared in the wake of the 1967 war, when for a moment it seemed as if Israel itself would be conquered and the experiment of a Jewish state ended. Instead, Israeli forces occupied the rest of the former Palestine mandate, territories known as the West Bank and the Gaza Strip. Most important was Israeli control of all of Jerusalem, including its eastern half, which held the Old City and sites of central importance to three faiths (Judaism, Islam, and Christianity). Buoyed by its triumphant victory, and by euphoric approval from the United States, Israel soon made the fateful decision to establish Jewish settlements in the occupied territories, outside the legal sovereignty of Israel itself. Washington occasionally lodged objections to this settlement policy, but did nothing to prevent it.

The next twelve years brought a series of events that drew the United States further into the region, sometimes in support of Israel and sometimes in opposition to the new phenomenon of Islamic fundamentalism. Another Arab-Israeli war came in 1973, which again ended with a resounding victory for Israel. Arab states reacted by imposing an oil embargo on the West and its allies, which triggered soaring energy prices and an economic crisis that had global consequences: these included an oil shortage and inflationary spiral in South Vietnam that led to its demise, and a massive stimulus to the sputtering planned economy of one of the world's largest oil producers, the Soviet Union. A second oil shock hit in 1979, following an even more momentous event: the Iranian Revolution. The authoritarian shah of Iran, who had enjoyed US backing ever since CIA agents helped orchestrate the coup in 1953 that had put him in power, fled in the face of rebelling Shiite fundamentalists. The theocratic state that took the shah's place encouraged protesters to seize control of the US embassy in Tehran, and over the next year and a half the Iranians held fifty-two Americans hostage. At the end of 1979, the Soviet Union invaded Afghanistan. Moscow's objective was to shore up a faltering client regime, but, in tandem with the Iranian Revolution, it appeared to President Jimmy Carter that US interests were being forced out of a critical region. The Carter Doctrine, proclaimed in January 1980, vowed to protect US access to the Persian Gulf, by force if necessary. As such, it was an update of the Open Door Notes that had put an indelible stamp on American globalism eighty years before.

The second (and final) Cold War

The Soviet invasion of Afghanistan not only sucked the United States deeper into the greater Middle East, it also brought a final end to détente. The Helsinki Accords had marked its peak but also, in hindsight, signaled its decline. Human-rights campaigners were wary of sacrificing American values on the altar of superpower stability and skeptical of Kissinger's plea that there was no higher human right than the freedom from nuclear annihilation. Despite Carter's robust response to events in Afghanistan, Ronald Reagan easily beat him in the 1980 presidential election on a promise to revive containment and, as one of his campaign slogans put it, "make America great again." Reagan increased military spending even as he cut taxes at home, which sent the world into a war scare and led to record federal budgetary deficits. In 1983, Reagan spoke of the USSR in a way no president since Truman had: as an "evil empire" that lay beyond the pale of civilization. Behind the scenes, a NATO military exercise codenamed Able Archer nearly led to the outbreak of war with the Soviet Union, which feared the exercise was a cover for an actual US attack.

After fifteen years of a hopeful but ultimately complacent period of détente, the second Cold War saw superpower tensions resume with a ferocity unmatched since the crisis years of the early 1960s. This repeated a familiar pattern. The period of 1979–84 marked a third phase of crisis of tensions, when the rest of the world trembled at the prospect of a third world war between Washington and Moscow (the others were 1947–53 and 1958–62). Like most complex systems, the Cold War ebbed and flowed in ways that were generally predictable, even if the specific circumstances were different. This time, however, the détente that followed the Second Cold War wasn't a temporary lull between crises, and the Cold War ended swiftly in 1989.

The world had two men to thank for this surprising turn of events. Foremost was Mikhail Gorbachev, who became leader of the Soviet Union in 1985 and immediately set about liberalizing the nation's political culture (*glasnost*) and reforming its creaking command economy (*perestroika*). This was just as revolutionary a transformation as Lenin had inaugurated in 1917, though reform, not revolution, was Gorbachev's goal; he never wanted to bring down the communist system in the Soviet Union, much less the Soviet Union itself. Gradual as they were, *glasnost* and *perestroika* were still too much of a shock to the system. They began a chain reaction that spread to the USSR's satellite states in Eastern Europe, and by 1989 the process had acquired a momentum that proved difficult to stop. The only way to do so would be with military force, as Gorbachev's predecessors hadn't hesitated to do (Khrushchev in Hungary in 1956 and Brezhnev in Czechoslovakia in 1968). But Gorbachev did hesitate when Eastern Europeans fled to Austria and West Germany and literally chipped away at the Berlin Wall. Although the Red Army had the power to stop it, Gorbachev refused to send it into action.

The other person who deserves praise for ending the Cold War peacefully is, perhaps more surprisingly, Ronald Reagan. This arch-cold warrior who relaunched America's moral crusade

10. When a new generation of Soviet leaders came to power in 1985, under the premiership of Mikhail Gorbachev, President Ronald Reagan changed course and sought a peaceful end to the Cold War. This photo of their 1988 summit meeting in Moscow captures the warmth of the new relationship.

against communism with bellicose rhetoric and higher military spending proved, in the end, to be one of the twentieth century's greatest peacemakers. That he was able to make peace almost entirely on American terms explains why he was so quickly apotheosized in the nation's collective memory.

Contrary to Cold War mythology, Reagan did not "bankrupt the Soviets" into submission, as many pundits would have it; nor did he "stare the communists down" with a cold warrior's toughness. The Soviet Union may have been in economic distress, but it was nowhere near insolvency. Even if it was, the Soviet military was still more than strong enough to suppress the burgeoning liberal movements in Eastern Europe. Had a reformer like Gorbachev not become Soviet leader in 1985, and had another hardliner been chosen instead, it's highly unlikely the Cold War would have ended in 1989–90, peacefully or not—indeed, it's likely the Soviet Union would still exist today. Gorbachev had a choice when he decided to launch *glasnost* and *perestroika*, and he had a choice when he decided not to crush the movements against communism in 1989. Nothing that happened in those four remarkable years between 1985 and 1989 was inevitable.

But Reagan had a choice, too, and it's to his everlasting credit that he decided to take Gorbachev at face value and negotiate with him as a partner for peace rather than as an enemy. Against the advice of many of his advisers, Reagan chose to accept Gorbachev's reforms as the best way forward, and he chose to meet Gorbachev at a series of summits—Geneva in 1985, Reykjavik in 1986, Washington in 1987, and Moscow and New York in 1988— designed to take the sting out of East-West tensions. The warmth these two leaders shared was obvious, and obviously sincere. Neither of them expected their new diplomacy to end the Cold War, but that's exactly what happened. For recognizing this opportunity and seizing it, Reagan deserves to go down in history alongside Gorbachev as a peacemaker.

There was no single endpoint to the Cold War, just as there had been no official start date in the late 1940s; it emerged through the accretion of structural forces, helped along at key moments by the choices of individuals, that crystallized into something much bigger. This is how it ended, too. The Berlin Wall came tumbling down in November 1989—after that, with Soviet power fundamentally compromised, it would have been difficult for the Cold War to continue as a bipolar struggle for supremacy between American liberal capitalism and Soviet communism. Divided Germany, the initial cause of Cold War tensions, reunified the following October. One after another, Communist rulers fell from power throughout Eastern Europe. The Warsaw Pact ended in July 1991, and in December the Soviet Union itself ceased to exist. The United States was now the world's only superpower. But as Americans would soon discover, supremacy rarely makes power easier to wield.

Chapter 6

Hyperpower and its discontents

[handwritten annotation: a condition of international anarchy faces power w/o (competitor) state under]

With the Cold War over, Americans were in a situation they hadn't faced since 1940—one in which their international existence wasn't defined in contrast to a totalitarian other. The situation of America in the world in 1991 was new in another way, too: the United States was in a position of supremacy unmatched since the days of the Roman Empire. It was now more than a superpower. Analysts referred to this condition as "unipolarity," a semantic illogicality that nonetheless captured the scale of American dominance after the bipolar Cold War had seen two superpowers share command of world affairs in nearly equal measure. Military strategists spoke more technically of America's "full spectrum dominance." American officials who believed they had the power to remake the world for the better, like Secretary of State Madeleine Albright, portrayed the United States as "the indispensable nation." Skeptics, by contrast, latched onto French Foreign Minister Hubert Védrine's label of "hyperpower," which connoted not just the scale of American power, but also its restless activism.

The era was perhaps best captured by two thoughtful (if flawed) observations of America and the world at an uncertain moment. In 1992, Francis Fukuyama, a Stanford social scientist, published *The End of History and the Last Man*, which argued that the denouement of the Cold War had ushered in the final phase of humanity's political development. Liberal democratic capitalism had seen off its many rivals, most notably fascism and communism, and now represented the only remaining plausible system of governance. From then on, Fukuyama predicted, liberalism, democracy, and capitalism would spread, and the world order would be embedded in the sanctity of individual rights.

History didn't quite turn out that way. The end of the Cold War did create space for Fukuyama's liberal democratic capitalism to thrive, but it also revived a set of dormant tensions fueled by race, religion, ethnicity, nation, and tribe. Once unleashed upon the world, these atavistic forces led to a new phase in history of renewed violence and bloodshed. Four years after Fukuyama had prematurely announced the end of history, his former graduate adviser, the Harvard political scientist Samuel Huntington, prophesied something much darker. In his 1996 book *The Clash of Civilizations and the Remaking of World Order*, Huntington warned that liberalism would not spread, but instead would have to fight for its life against an onslaught of resurgent nationalism, ethnic pride, and religious fundamentalism.

Fukuyama's future looked bright, Huntington's bleak; they seemed mutually exclusive. But both visions were at once correct and incorrect. After the Cold War, liberalism was triumphant even as, simultaneously, other challenges arose. The chaotic world since the end of the Cold War has been shaped by the contest between these two visions, and America's role in the world has been buffeted by their violent struggle.

Forever wars

The transition in US foreign policy toward the Middle East was happening already before the end of the Cold War, but the dramatic events of 1989–91 accelerated it. The critical importance of the region stemmed from a combination of several factors. One was the economic and strategic importance of oil. The United States became a net importer of oil in the 1970s, and most US allies in Europe and Japan had long been reliant on foreign oil; at the same time, key states of the Middle East, notably Saudi Arabia, Iraq, and Iran, became some of the world's biggest exporters. Another reason was the region's geostrategic importance, particularly in a new age of globalization, when access to energy supplies and sea lanes between Asia and Europe was vital. A third reason was the rise of Islamic terrorism, an issue of perennial crisis that, in American political culture, came to rival the Cold War in its durable intensity. The fourth reason was rooted in domestic politics as well as geopolitics: Israel. Since 1967, Israel and the United States had been growing closer. Israel was a critical ally first against communism, and then against terrorism. But it was also important to a wide range of Americans, not just Jews, as a symbol of liberal democracy in a region of the world where liberalism and democracy were rarities.

On their own, none of these reasons can explain the importance of the Middle East to the United States. But in combination, especially as they grew over time in size and momentum, the four factors above created the conditions for a nearly permanent state of US crisis intervention in the region.

When Iraq invaded Kuwait in August 1990, the United States assembled an international coalition in response. The result was the 1991 Gulf War, which saw the United States oust Iraqi forces from Kuwait. Iraq's leader, Saddam Hussein, was allowed to remain in power, albeit under the strict constraints—officially sanctioned by the UN but enforced by the United States—of limited air sovereignty, disarmament, an economic embargo aimed at curtailing Iraqi oil revenues, the eradication of Iraq's weapons of mass destruction (WMD) programs, and a semi-autonomous Kurdish region in the north of the country. Saddam Hussein chafed under these restrictions, and signaled—misleadingly, as it turned out—that he had not, in fact, dismantled his WMD capabilities.

Defeating Iraq meant the liberation of Kuwait and the safeguarding of Saudi Arabia, but this also brought the United States into a more intimate relationship with a region undergoing a profoundly destabilizing religious revolution. The Iranian Revolution of 1979 and the Islamic resistance to the Soviet invasion of Afghanistan that same year had been a foretaste of what Samuel Huntington had predicted would happen with the end of the Cold War: the explosive reemergence of religious strife. When the United States—a complex modern society that was simultaneously devoutly Christian, notably Jewish, and relentlessly secular—began playing a more intimate role in Muslim countries like Saudi Arabia, a faction of hardcore Sunni fundamentalists mounted a resistance.

people naturally went against it

The most notable anti-American group to emerge called itself al-Qaeda—"the foundation" in Arabic, which hints at the group's doctrinal purity. Al-Qaeda was led by a charismatic Saudi, Osama bin Laden, who came from a wealthy family but had grown disillusioned with the West and its support for Arab regimes in the Middle East that collaborated with the United States, and thus, to his mind, betrayed the sacred principles of Islam. As a member of the mujahideen, bin Laden had fought the Soviets in Afghanistan in the 1980s. When that war ended in 1989, he took the fight to the Americans. Both campaigns, bin Laden claimed, were holy wars against the forces of modernism that aimed to subjugate Islam; he made little distinction between communist Russians and capitalist Americans.

against American foreign involvement

→ great negative impact

Al-Qaeda and its affiliates mounted several attacks against US targets in the 1990s, including the bombing of the World Trade Center in New York in 1993; the destruction of the US embassies in Kenya and Tanzania in 1998; and a deadly 200 attack on an American warship, the USS *Cole*, that was docked at a harbor in Yemen. But their biggest operation, one that caused a violent shift in history similar to the impact the Japanese attack on Pearl Harbor had in 1941, is simply known as "9/11." It came on

Forms of racism
"all to
once"

have

September 11, 2001, when al-Qaeda fighters hijacked four civilian airplanes and crashed two of them into the World Trade Center and one into the Pentagon. President George W. Bush responded by launching an open-ended "global war on terror," which targeted not only non-state terrorist groups like al-Qaeda, but also states that were suspected of aiding and abetting terrorism.

The first state to fall afoul of this doctrine was Afghanistan, where al-Qaeda was based. Bush demanded that the Taliban, the group that ruled Afghanistan, turn over bin Laden. When the Taliban refused, the United States invaded the country in October. The Taliban fled the capital, Kabul, and bin Laden went into hiding (he was eventually killed by US special forces in Pakistan in 2011). It seemed the United States had won the war, but it found occupying Afghanistan much more difficult than conquering its capital, and a war of pacification quickly stalemated into an indefinite and indeterminate struggle for control of the country. Afghanistan was a difficult nation to occupy, as the British found out in the nineteenth century and the Soviets discovered in the 1980s. But the Bush administration compounded these inherent difficulties with errors of its own.

Toward the end of 2001, with victory in Afghanistan seemingly secured, Bush secretly turned his attention to a more familiar adversary: Iraq. Members of the Bush administration, notably in the Pentagon, suspected Iraq not only of maintaining a clandestine and illegal WMD program, but also of supporting al-Qaeda. There was no evidence to support either theory, but that mattered little in the fearful atmosphere created by 9/11. Some of the more aggressive members of the Bush administration also saw a moment of opportunity to implement their own visions of US dominance in the region. As a result, the United States invaded Iraq in March 2003, a dozen years after first entering the country, in a now-familiar pattern: a quick and apparently easy march to the capital, Baghdad, followed by a bloody and chaotic occupation in the face of a highly effective insurgency. The anti-American campaign only began to quieten in the fall of 2007, over four years after the initial invasion, but when US troops left in 2011, Iraq was no more peaceful or stable than it had been in 2001. In fact, a new Sunni extremist movement, the Islamic State of Iraq and Syria (ISIS), took advantage of the chaos and mounted a new insurgency against both the occupation forces and the government in Baghdad.

→ Negative representation of civil society

New responsibilities

The decade following the collapse of the Soviet Union earned the awkward but entirely fitting term of "the post-Cold War era." The 1990s were post-Cold War both in the literal sense that these years followed the end of the Cold War, and in the figurative sense that they saw the end of one of the Cold War's defining features: shared global power between the United States and the USSR. In the post-Cold War era, only the United States remained.

As a result, the United States towered over all others, and indeed over the international system itself. In this unusual moment—with Russia prostrate, the Japanese economy entering its lost decade, and China only just beginning to gain strength—Americans faced no rivals. Washington took advantage of the situation to remake the world in its image. With Fukuyama's triumphalism legitimating their efforts, US officials and intellectuals promoted the spread of liberal democratic capitalism around the world—not just for the good of people everywhere, but for the security of the United States. According to "the democratic peace," an academic theory that became fashionable in Washington, liberal democracies don't launch wars of aggression and don't go to war with one another. The spread of democracies would therefore also ensure the spread of peace. With this in mind, the administration of President Bill Clinton defined its strategy as moving "from containment to enlargement" of "the world's free community of market democracies." Spreading "freedom" became an American gospel.

Believed that democracies get along with other democracies

This Fukuyamian optimism about the power of international liberalism took such powerful hold in the American official mind that it quickly became known as "the Washington consensus." America's leverage came mostly during moments of macroeconomic crisis when other countries needed urgent financial assistance, such as the Mexican currency crisis of 1994, the Southeast Asian financial panic of 1997, and the Argentinian and Russian currency crises of 1998. In exchange for a bailout, afflicted countries had to undertake "structural adjustment" by deregulating and privatizing their economies. At the same time, the United States experienced a surge of immigration from Latin America (especially Mexico), South Asia, China, and Southeast Asia (mainly the Philippines but also Vietnam) that deepened the globalization not only of the US economy, but of American society itself.

Fukuyama's optimism was soon tempered by the coldly realistic pessimism of Huntington's clash of civilizations, which began unfolding just as the Washington consensus was becoming conventional wisdom. "Ethnic cleansing"—a new term that differed from genocide in that it aimed to clear out certain ethnic groups from a particular space of contested territory—erupted in southeastern Europe, as Yugoslavia broke apart into warring factions. The former Yugoslav republic of Bosnia and Herzegovina, with its intermingled communities of Catholic Croats, Orthodox Serbs, and Muslim Bosniaks, saw the worst cases of ethnic cleaning, but it was not unique. Genocidal violence also broke out in Rwanda, in 1994, as the Hutu majority indiscriminately slaughtered up to a million members of a rival tribe, the Tutsi.

To solve the problems of the post-Cold War world, the visions of Fukuyama and Huntington formed an admixture known variously as "liberal interventionism," "humanitarian interventionism," or the "responsibility to protect" (often known as "R2P"). Fukuyama's liberal triumphalism identified the course of history; Huntington's civilizational fatalism identified the primordial forces that were standing in history's way. The solution, then, was to mobilize the former against the latter, with liberal democracies using their political, economic, and ultimately military power to defeat the anti-historical forces of religious, ethnic, and nationalist violence.

The result was a new ideological justification for foreign wars, not unlike the liberal imperialism of earlier centuries, by which the United States and its allies (most notably Britain) would intervene in other countries for their own good as well as the security of others. It was, officials in Washington, New York, London, and Brussels believed, America's responsibility to use its power to protect the powerless, even if that meant violating a much older principle of international law, national sovereignty. Clinton's failure to intervene in Rwanda only made this new doctrine all the more compelling—the haunting image of thousands of dead Tutsis floating down the Kagera River loomed large in the Western imagination. With this in mind, the United States mobilized NATO to stop the bloodshed in the Balkans, first in Bosnia in 1995 and then in Kosovo in 1999. Other interventions in West Africa and, in 2011, Libya were justified as the West's responsibility to protect other nations and peoples.

A new Cold War?

Within fifteen years of the Cold War's end, the unipolar moment of American supremacy was on the wane. Partly this was due to the Bush administration's strategically disastrous response to 9/11, which ultimately failed in Iraq. But it was also the inevitable result of the normal course of international relations. Even if the United States remained the world's most powerful state, other nations were bound to narrow the gap. And in the twenty-first century, the country that did the most catching up was the People's Republic of China.

When Richard Nixon traveled to Beijing in 1972 he knew he was opening up a new chapter in world history, but even he would probably be surprised to see just how momentous the change has been. Within three decades, China went from being a large but impoverished nation to an economic powerhouse with enough military clout to rival that of the United States, at least in East Asia and the western Pacific. ~ ?

rival superpowers

Ironically, America did the most to help China along its new path. At first, in between Nixon's opening and the end of the Cold War, China was a strategic ally against a mutual enemy, the Soviet Union. But money soon provided the bond. In the 1980s, under the post-Mao leadership of Deng Xiaoping, China adopted a state-managed market economy while also preserving the Communist Party's monopoly on political power. Once the Cold War ended, the Chinese economy prospered in its role as sweatshop to the world, producing consumer goods more efficiently and cheaply, and on a grander scale, than anywhere else. Americans encouraged the Chinese economic miracle, not only because it provided US consumers with quality products at low cost, but because it seemed to herald China's eventual acceptance of the Washington consensus. China became a member of the World Trade Organization in late 2001, right at the moment when the United States, flush from victory in Afghanistan and setting its sites on Iraq, seemed dominant.

In retrospect, that moment marked an important watershed. In Iraq and Afghanistan, the United States suffered a series of humiliating defeats. Then in 2008, an economic downturn severe enough to earn the nickname "the Great Recession" destroyed what was left of American claims to primacy. Over the same period, however, the Chinese economy continued to grow, surpassing Japan to become the world's second-largest in 2010. Crucially, Beijing had been translating that economic power into domestic political stability and international military power. It spent billions of dollars on bilateral aid and infrastructure programs throughout Asia, Africa, and Latin America, and constructed a series of offshore military bases from reclaimed land in the disputed waters of the South China Sea.

In a speech to the Australian parliament in 2011, President Barack Obama announced that the United States would pivot away from the Middle East and toward East Asia so that China's rise could be tamed and confined. This made strategic sense, as the center of gravity of world politics and the global economy had shifted eastward at a moment when it had become all too clear that US military power had only had very large negative consequences in the Middle East. Yet geopolitical realities proved stubborn: extrication from the Middle East proved difficult, and it was clear that China had risen too far, too fast, to be tamed or confined. Whatever the merits of US or Chinese ambitions, the rivalry between Beijing and Washington is certain to define international relations for decades to come. Whether it will be a peaceful rivalry or lead to military conflict is the biggest strategic issue facing the world in the early twenty-first century.

The outcome of the Sino-American struggle will also probably determine the global fate of liberal norms and free-market economies. The promotion and protection of liberal democratic capitalism has been the lodestar for America in the world for over a century now, from the Open Door Notes of 1899–1900 to the Washington consensus, humanitarian interventionism, and beyond. The era since 2001 has been one of almost continual crisis for the United States; by contrast, China has gone from strength to strength. And yet, despite self-inflicted wounds like the calamitous, needless wars in Iraq and Libya, and despite the severity of the Great Recession, the United States is still the world's preeminent state. It retains most of its cultural soft power, and it remains the world's economic engine, leading technological innovator, and, by some distance, dominant military power. Whether the next hundred years will be another American century, or the Chinese century, has yet to be determined.

Fight over who holds the power in the world

Further reading

General works

Costigliola, Frank, and Michael J. Hogan. *Explaining the History of American Foreign Relations*, 3rd ed. Cambridge: Cambridge University Press, 2016.

Cumings, Bruce. *Dominion from Sea to Sea: Pacific Ascendancy and American Power*. New Haven, CT: Yale University Press, 2009.

Gabaccia, Donna R. *Foreign Relations: American Immigration in Global Perspective*. Princeton, NJ: Princeton University Press, 2012.

Herring, George. *The American Century and Beyond: U.S. Foreign Relations, 1893–2014*. New York: Oxford University Press, 2017.

Herring, George. *From Colony to Superpower: U.S. Foreign Relations since 1776*. New York: Oxford University Press, 2008.

Herring, George. *Years of Peril and Ambition: U.S. Foreign Relations, 1776–1921*. New York: Oxford University Press, 2017.

Hopkins, A. G. *American Empire: A Global History*. Princeton, NJ: Princeton University Press, 2018.

Hunt, Michael H. *Ideology and U.S. Foreign Policy*. New Haven, CT: Yale University Press, 1987, 2009.

Kaplan, Amy. *The Anarchy of Empire in the Making of U.S. Culture*. Cambridge, MA: Harvard University Press, 2002.

Mayers, David. *Dissenting Voices in America's Rise to Power*. Cambridge: Cambridge University Press, 2007.

McDougall, Walter A. *Promised Land, Crusader State: The American Encounter with the World since 1776*. New York: Houghton Mifflin, 1997.

Preston, Andrew. *Sword of the Spirit, Shield of Faith: Religion in American War and Diplomacy*. New York: Alfred A. Knopf, 2012.

Stephanson, Anders. *Manifest Destiny: American Expansion and the Empire of Right*. New York: Hill and Wang, 1995.

Tyrrell, Ian. *Transnational Nation: United States History in Global Perspective since 1789*. New York: Red Globe Press, 2007, 2015.

Williams, William Appleman. *The Tragedy of American Diplomacy*. Cleveland: World Pub. Co., 1959; New York: W. W. Norton, 2009.

Founding and early republic

Calloway, Colin G. *The Indian World of George Washington: The First President, the First Americans, and the Birth of the Nation*. New York: Oxford University Press, 2018.

Fitz, Caitlin. *Our Sister Republics: The United States in an Age of American Revolutions*. New York: Liveright, 2016.

Gould, Eliga H. *Among the Powers of the Earth: The American Revolution and the Making of a New World Empire*. Cambridge, MA: Harvard University Press, 2012.

Hendrickson, David C. *Peace Pact: The Lost World of the American Founding*. Lawrence: University Press of Kansas, 2003.

Taylor, Alan. *American Revolutions: A Continental History, 1750–1804*. New York: W. W. Norton, 2016.

Nineteenth-century expansionism

Blackhawk, Ned. *Violence over the Land: Indians and Empires in the Early American West*. Cambridge, MA: Harvard University Press, 2006.

Conroy-Krutz, Emily. *Christian Imperialism: Converting the World in the Early American Republic*. Ithaca, NY: Cornell University Press, 2015.

DeLay, Brian. *War of a Thousand Deserts: Indian Raids and the U.S.-Mexican War*. New Haven, CT: Yale University Press, 2008.

Greenberg, Amy S. *A Wicked War: Polk, Clay, Lincoln, and the 1846 U.S. Invasion of Mexico*. New York: Alfred A. Knopf, 2012.

Guyatt, Nicholas. *Bind Us Apart: How Enlightened Americans Invented Racial Segregation*. New York: Basic Books, 2016.

Hahn, Steven. *A Nation without Borders: The United States and Its World in an Age of Civil Wars, 1830–1910*. New York: Penguin Books, 2016.

Jacobs, Margaret D. *White Mother to a Dark Race: Settler Colonialism, Maternalism, and the Removal of Indigenous Children in the American West and Australia, 1880–1940*. Lincoln: University of Nebraska Press, 2009.

Lee, Robert. "Accounting for Conquest: The Price of the Louisiana Purchase of Indian Country." *Journal of American History* 103 (March 2017): 921–942.

Nugent, Walter. *Habits of Empire: A History of American Expansionism*. New York: Alfred A. Knopf, 2008.

Rothman, Adam. *Slave Country: American Expansion and the Origins of the Deep South*. Cambridge, MA: Harvard University Press, 2005.

Sexton, Jay. *The Monroe Doctrine: Empire and Nation in Nineteenth-Century America*. New York: Hill and Wang, 2011.

Twentieth century: overviews and interpretations

de Grazia, Victoria. *Irresistible Empire: America's Advance through Twentieth-Century Europe*. Cambridge, MA: Harvard University Press, 2005.

Dudziak, Mary L. *War Time: An Idea, Its History, Its Consequences*. New York: Oxford University Press, 2012.

Engel, Jeffrey A., Mark Atwood Lawrence, and Andrew Preston, eds. *America in the World: A History in Documents from the War with Spain to the War on Terror*. Princeton, NJ: Princeton University Press, 2014.

Immerwahr, Daniel. *How to Hide an Empire: A History of the Greater United States*. New York: Farrar, Straus and Giroux, 2019.

Latham, Michael E. *The Right Kind of Revolution: Modernization, Development, and U.S. Foreign Policy from the Cold War to the Present*. Ithaca, NY: Cornell University Press, 2011.

Leffler, Melvyn P. *Safeguarding Democratic Capitalism: U.S. Foreign Policy and National Security, 1920–2015*. Princeton, NJ: Princeton University Press, 2017.

McAlister, Melani. *Epic Encounters: Culture, Media, and U.S. Interests in the Middle East since 1945*. Berkeley: University of California Press, 2005.

Milne, David. *Worldmaking: The Art and Science of American Diplomacy*. New York: Farrar, Straus and Giroux, 2015.

Nichols, Christopher McKnight. *Promise and Peril: America at the Dawn of a Global Age*. Cambridge, MA: Harvard University Press, 2011.

Rosenberg, Emily S. *Spreading the American Dream: American Economic and Cultural Expansion, 1890–1945*. New York: Hill and Wang, 1982.

Sherry, Michael S. *In the Shadow of War: The United States since the 1930s*. New Haven, CT: Yale University Press, 1995.

Thompson, John A. *A Sense of Power: The Roots of America's Global Role*. Ithaca, NY: Cornell University Press, 2015.

Zelizer, Julian E. *Arsenal of Democracy: The Politics of National Security—From World War II to the War on Terrorism*. New York: Basic Books, 2010.

War and empire after 1898

Hoganson, Kristin L. *Fighting for American Manhood: How Gender Politics Provoked the Spanish-American and Philippine-American Wars*. New Haven, CT: Yale University Press, 1998.

Kramer, Paul A. *The Blood of Government: Race, Empire, the United States, and the Philippines*. Chapel Hill: University of North Carolina Press, 2006.

LaFeber, Walter. *The New Empire: An Interpretation of American Expansion, 1860–1898*. Ithaca, NY: Cornell University Press, 1963.

Perez Jr., Louis A. *The War of 1898: The United States and Cuba in History and Historiography*. Chapel Hill: University of North Carolina Press, 1998.

Renda, Mary A. *Taking Haiti: Military Occupation and the Culture of U.S. Imperialism, 1915–1940*. Chapel Hill: University of North Carolina Press, 2001.

World War I era

Capozzola, Christopher. *Uncle Sam Wants You: World War I and the Making of the Modern American Citizen*. New York: Oxford University Press, 2008.

Epstein, Katherine C. *Torpedo: Inventing the Military-Industrial Complex in the United States and Great Britain*. Cambridge, MA: Harvard University Press, 2014.

Irwin, Julia F. *Making the World Safe: The American Red Cross and a Nation's Humanitarian Awakening*. New York: Oxford University Press, 2013.

Keene, Jennifer D. *Doughboys, the Great War, and the Remaking of America*. Baltimore: Johns Hopkins University Press, 2003.

American Foreign Relations

Kennedy, Ross A. *The Will To Believe: Woodrow Wilson, World War I, and America's Strategy for Peace and Security*. Kent, OH: Kent State University Press, 2009.

Knock, Thomas J. *To End All Wars: Woodrow Wilson and the Quest for a New World Order*. Princeton, NJ: Princeton University Press, 1992.

Manela, Erez. *The Wilsonian Moment: Self-Determination and the International Origins of Anticolonial Nationalism*. New York: Oxford University Press, 2007.

Tooze, Adam. *The Deluge: The Great War, America and the Remaking of the Global Order, 1916–1931*. New York: Penguin, 2014.

World War II era

Blower, Brooke L. "From Isolationism to Neutrality: A New Framework for Understanding American Political Culture, 1919–1941." *Diplomatic History* 38 (April 2014): 345–376.

Borgwardt, Elizabeth. *A New Deal for the World: America's Vision for Human Rights*. Cambridge, MA: Harvard University Press, 2005.

Dallek, Robert. *Franklin D. Roosevelt and American Foreign Policy, 1932–1945*. New York: Oxford University Press, 1995.

Doenecke, Justus D. *Storm on the Horizon: The Challenge to American Intervention, 1939–1941*. Lanham, MD: Rowman & Littlefield, 2000.

Kimball, Warren F. *The Juggler: Franklin Roosevelt as Wartime Statesman*. Princeton, NJ: Princeton University Press, 1994.

Reynolds, David. *From Munich to Pearl Harbor: Roosevelt's America and the Origins of the Second World War*. Chicago: Ivan R. Dee, 2001.

Cold War: overviews

Borstelmann, Thomas. *The Cold War and the Color Line: American Race Relations in the Global Arena*. Cambridge, MA: Harvard University Press, 2001.

Chamberlin, Paul Thomas. *The Cold War's Killing Fields: Rethinking the Long Peace*. New York: HarperCollins, 2018.

Craig, Campbell, and Fredrik Logevall. *America's Cold War: The Politics of Insecurity*. Cambridge, MA: Harvard University Press, 2009.

Gaddis, John Lewis. *Strategies of Containment: A Critical Appraisal of American National Security Policy during the Cold War*. New York: Oxford University Press, 2005.

Gaddis, John Lewis. *We Now Know: Rethinking Cold War History*. Oxford: Oxford University Press, 1997.

Isaac, Joel, and Duncan Bell, eds. *Uncertain Empire: American History and the Idea of the Cold War*. New York: Oxford University Press, 2012.

Kwon, Heonik. *The Other Cold War*. New York: Columbia University Press, 2010.

Leebaert, Derek. *The Fifty-Year Wound: How America's Cold War Victory Has Shaped Our World*. Boston: Little, Brown, 2002.

Leffler, Melvyn P., and Odd Arne Westad, eds. *The Cambridge History of the Cold War*, 3 vols. Cambridge: Cambridge University Press, 2010.

Leffler, Melvyn P. *For the Soul of Mankind: The United States, the Soviet Union, and the Cold War*. New York: Hill and Wang, 2007.

Reynolds, David. *One World Divisible: A Global History Since 1945*. New York: W. W. Norton, 2000.

Westad, Odd Arne. *The Cold War: A World History*. New York: Basic Books, 2017.

Westad, Odd Arne. *The Global Cold War: Third World Interventions and the Making of Our Times*. Cambridge: Cambridge University Press, 2005.

Cold War: case studies

Anderson, Carol. *Eyes Off the Prize: The United Nations and the African American Struggle for Human Rights, 1944–1955*. Cambridge: Cambridge University Press, 2003.

Dudziak, Mary L. *Cold War Civil Rights: Race and the Image of American Democracy*. Princeton, NJ: Princeton University Press, 2000.

Freedman, Lawrence. *Kennedy's Wars: Berlin, Cuba, Laos, and Vietnam*. New York: Oxford University Press, 2000.

Fursenko, Aleksandr, and Timothy J. Naftali. *One Hell of a Gamble: Khrushchev, Castro, and Kennedy, 1958–1964*. New York: W. W. Norton, 1997.

Hitchcock, William I. *The Age of Eisenhower: America and the World in the 1950s*. New York: Simon & Schuster, 2018.

Leffler, Melvyn P. *A Preponderance of Power: National Security, the Truman Administration, and the Cold War*. Stanford: Stanford University Press, 1992.

Rotter, Andrew J. *Comrades at Odds: The United States and India, 1947–1964*. Ithaca, NY: Cornell University Press, 2000.

Stueck, William. *Rethinking the Korean War: A New Diplomatic and Strategic History*. Princeton: Princeton University Press, 2002.

Vietnam

Asselin, Pierre. *Vietnam's American War: A History*. Cambridge: Cambridge University Press, 2018.

Bradley, Mark Philip. *Vietnam at War*. Oxford: Oxford University Press, 2009.

Daddis, Gregory A. *Westmoreland's War: Reassessing American Strategy in Vietnam*. New York: Oxford University Press, 2014.

Daddis, Gregory A. *Withdrawal: Reassessing America's Final Years in Vietnam*. New York: Oxford University Press, 2017.

Lawrence, Mark Atwood. *The Vietnam War: A Concise International History*. New York: Oxford University Press, 2008.

Logevall, Fredrik. *Choosing War: The Lost Chance for Peace and the Escalation of War in Vietnam*. Berkeley: University of California Press, 1999.

Logevall, Fredrik. *Embers of War: The Fall of an Empire and the Making of America's Vietnam*. New York: Random House, 2012.

Nguyen, Lien-Hang T. *Hanoi's War: An International History of the War for Peace in Vietnam*. Chapel Hill: University of North Carolina Press, 2012.

Preston, Andrew. *The War Council: McGeorge Bundy, the NSC, and Vietnam*. Cambridge, MA: Harvard University Press, 2006.

The Cold War after Vietnam

Borstelmann, Thomas. *The 1970s: A New Global History from Civil Rights to Economic Inequality*. Princeton, NJ: Princeton University Press, 2012.

Brands, Hal. *Making the Unipolar Moment: U.S. Foreign Policy and the Rise of the Post-Cold War Order*. Ithaca, NY: Cornell University Press, 2016.

Del Pero, Mario. *The Eccentric Realist: Henry Kissinger and the Shaping of American Foreign Policy.* Ithaca, NY: Cornell University Press, 2010.

Logevall, Fredrik, and Andrew Preston, eds. *Nixon in the World: American Foreign Relations, 1969–1977.* New York: Oxford University Press, 2008.

Morgan, Michael Cotey. *The Final Act: The Helsinki Accords and the Transformation of the Cold War.* Princeton, NJ: Princeton University Press, 2018.

Moyn, Samuel. *The Last Utopia: Human Rights in History.* Cambridge, MA: Harvard University Press, 2010.

Sargent, Daniel J. *A Superpower Transformed: The Remaking of American Foreign Relations in the 1970s.* New York: Oxford University Press, 2015.

Snyder, Sarah B. *Human Rights Activism and the End of the Cold War: A Transnational History of the Helsinki Network.* Cambridge: Cambridge University Press, 2011.

From the end of the Cold War to the "War on Terror"

Bacevich, Andrew J. *America's War for the Greater Middle East: A Military History.* New York: Random House, 2016.

Bailey, Beth, and Richard H. Immerman, eds. *Understanding the U.S. Wars in Iraq and Afghanistan.* New York: NYU Press, 2015.

Chandrasekaran, Rajiv. *Imperial Life in The Emerald City: Inside Iraq's Green Zone.* New York: Alfred A. Knopf, 2006.

Chandrasekaran, Rajiv. *Little America: The War Within the War for Afghanistan.* New York: Alfred A. Knopf, 2012.

Chollet, Derek, and James Goldgeier. *America Between the Wars: From 11/9 to 9/11.* New York: Public Affairs, 2008.

Coll, Steve. *Directorate S: The C.I.A. and America's Secret Wars in Afghanistan and Pakistan.* New York: Penguin Press, 2018.

Coll, Steve. *Ghost Wars: The Secret History of the CIA, Afghanistan, and Bin Laden, from the Soviet Invasion to September 10, 2001.* New York: Penguin Books, 2004.

Engel, Jeffrey A. *When the World Seemed New: George H. W. Bush and the End of the Cold War.* New York: Houghton Mifflin Harcourt, 2017.

Fuller, Christopher J. *See It/Shoot It: The Secret History of the CIA's Lethal Drone Program.* New Haven, CT: Yale University Press, 2017.

Mann, James. *Rise of the Vulcans: The History of Bush's War Cabinet.* New York: Viking, 2004.

Mann, James. *The Obamians: The Struggle Inside the White House to Redefine American Power.* New York: Viking, 2012.

Packer, George. *The Assassins' Gate: America in Iraq.* New York: Farrar, Straus and Giroux, 2005.

Ricks, Thomas E. *Fiasco: The American Military Adventure in Iraq.* New York: Penguin, 2006.

Wright, Lawrence. *The Looming Tower: Al-Qaeda and the Road to 9/11.* New York: Alfred A. Knopf, 2006.

Index

Index

Index

American Foreign Relations